Beyond The Kitchen

A DREAMERS GUIDE

Thomas Cowan

A QUARTO BOOK

RUNNING PRESS
BOOK PUBLISHERS
PHILADELPHIA, PENNSYLVANIA

A RUNNING PRESS/QUARTO BOOK
Copyright © 1985 by Quarto Marketing Ltd.

9 8 7 6 5 4 3 2 1
Digit on the right indicates the number of this printing.

Library of Congress Cataloging in Publication Number:
84-042923

ISBN 0-89471-303-5 (cloth)
ISBN 0-89471-306-X (paperback)
ISBN 0-89471-304-3 (library binding)

BEYOND THE KITCHEN was produced and prepared by
Quarto Marketing Ltd.
15 West 26th Street, New York, NY 10010

Editor: Karla Olson
Managing Editor: Naomi Black
Art Director: Richard Boddy
Designer: Abby Kagan/Mary Moriarty
Photo Research: Susan Duane
U.K. Photo Research: Sylvia Katz

Typeset by BPE Graphics, Inc.
Color separations by Hong Kong Scanner Craft Company Ltd.
Printed and bound in Hong Kong by Leefung-Asco Printers Ltd.

This book may be ordered from the publisher.
Please include $1.00 postage.
But try your bookstore first.

Running Press Book Publishers
125 South 22nd Street
Philadelphia, Pennsylvania 19103

<u>Cover Photograph</u>
Photographer: Jaime Ardiles-Arce
Designer: Juan Mir, A.S.I.D.

ABOUT THE AUTHOR

Thomas Cowan, author of *Beyond the Bath: A Dreamer's Guide*, is a widely published freelance writer of diverse interests; his specialties include home and personal improvement. Among the books he has written are *Great Kids Rooms, The Home Security Guide, How to Remove Spots and Stains, Free Things for Homeowners,* and *How to Tap into Your Own Genius.* He holds a Ph.D. in history and literature from St. Louis University, has taught humanities on a college level, and is an award-winning poet.

Contents

While this kitchen may look all white at the moment, imagine yourself preparing a leafy green salad with red ripe tomatoes. Radishes, dark green cucumbers, and bright orange carrots would throw splashes of brilliant color into this monochromatic area. In kitchens such as this one, the food definitely becomes the center of attention, and visitors can easily see the primary purpose of the room. With professional seriousness, the cook in this setting can focus totally on the job at hand, and because it is so easy to see what you're doing and what the final dish will look like, chances are any meal will be easier and more fun to prepare.

Introduction

*N*o matter what its design or location in the home, the kitchen will always be the focal point of a family's life. We are called to it several times a day when hunger nudges us for full, hearty meals or between-time snacks. We hear the refrigerator door close, a water tap turn on, a chair scrape along the floor as it is pulled out from the table, and we know that the kitchen has once again come to life. Someone is there; food is being prepared; conversation ensues. Again we can experience the joy of sharing our lives with those we love in a room redolent with fond memories of food and drink, family, laughter, and tears.

The kitchens of today—and those now being designed for tomorrow—are a direct link from kitchens in the past, for the fundamentals always remain the same. People for generations before us prepared and ate meals and enjoyed each other's company in similar surroundings. New materials are created by innovative manufacturers; improved appliances are designed by imaginative engineers; and startling arrangements are introduced by bold designers. But through all this novelty and growth we can still recognize the basic ingredients. Unusual design breakthroughs may be breathtaking, new acquisitions may surprise and amuse us, but underneath it all, we still anticipate the mouth-watering dinner or the nourishing breakfast that we hope is as good for us as food was in earlier days when sustenance came more directly from the land to the table.

Modern kitchens, like those of the past, are used for many more activities and rituals than just those associated with food. They are still the multipurpose rooms that must accommodate everyone's needs—that must be ready for unannounced visits, impromptu card games, homework sessions, and lingering family conversations. Most families no longer make a distinction between what is a proper kitchen activity and what is not. Everything can be—and is—done in today's kitchen. The shapes of appliances and furniture, the colors and textures of the room, the changes in lighting all contribute to an environment that is aesthetically pleasing as well as functionally versatile. In planning a kitchen we must let our imagination mull through both traditional and nontraditional kitchen activities because, of all the rooms in the house, this is the one that the family will use the most frequently and feel most at home in.

The world beyond the kitchen eventually finds its way into the kitchen. For instance, this room often welcomes visitors more invitingly than the entrance foyer or the living room. In fact, by its very nature, the kitchen cannot keep life out. On the contrary, people flow through the kitchen many times a day, for all sorts of reasons—to eat, drink, complete a task, or just relax there. Lucky is the household that enjoys a large, spacious kitchen, carefully designed to accommodate the numerous plans and purposes this room cannot escape. Fortunate are the housekeepers whose kitchens utilize the latest labor-saving appliances and easy-to-clean materials so that the chores that are part and parcel of most kitchen activities can be performed swiftly and easily.

Creating decorative touches for a kitchen is often a home designer's favorite task. This room, perhaps more than any other, is the most challenging and satisfying to design and appoint. It can be filled with a multitude of gadgets, specialized furniture, and appliances; a marvelous array of styles and strategies for the usual accessories of any room—curtains, lights, floor coverings—can be devised to complete it; a plethora of strategies can be devised to incorporate imaginative extras. In fact, some kitchen supply shops and accessory boutiques are veritable jungles of gifts, furnishings, accouterments, and bright ideas. What's more, kitchens can be as eclectic as the owner desires, incorporating traditional styles and patterns with the very modern.

We invite you into the gallery of kitchens we have selected for this volume, hoping that in each you will experience what designers and homeowners have discovered in creating them—that the kitchen is a fun and surprising place, that it serves the creative imagination with infinite possibilities just as it can faithfully serve three balanced meals a day. Some of our selections will please you more than others. Some will defy many of your preconceived notions of what a kitchen should be. Others will astound you with bold, imaginative displays that can be adapted to your own family's needs. In any case, we hope that all of them stir up dreams of what an exceptional spot your kitchen can be—a place that becomes uniquely and distinctively your own when you garnish it with as much love and imagination as you use for the special meals you enjoy there.

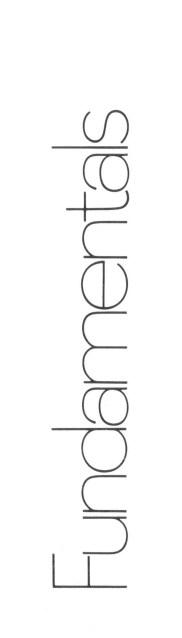

1

Fundamentals

Here's proof that light gray has a dignified splendor all its own. Rather than being dull and drab as so many people imagine gray to be, this kitchen testifies to the shimmering elegance that can be achieved when one muted color is handled with loving care. Notice the slightly darker gray tone on the crossribs of the cabinetry, producing a contrast that is subtle yet clearly visible. To match the restrained contrast in tone with that in texture and shape, this designer played off the speckled marbled floor, countertops, and backsplash with smooth, clear surfaces on cabinet doors and drawers. The entire room is a gentle play of concave and convex curvatures that produce especially beautiful reflections.

Our memories are redolent with sense impressions—light cracking through bedroom windows, the chatter of grownups behind closed doors, the evening breezes cooling the porch at dusk. And then there are the smells and fragrances that meet us at every corner of our lives. The best aromas arising from anyone's childhood memories are those that drifted from the kitchen on baking days and wafted down hallways, through the rest of the house, and upstairs into bedrooms where we read books or played with crayons and our favorite toys. Remember how quickly we scampered downstairs to discover what good things were baking in the oven? Remember how we knew immediately on arriving home after school that mother had made Tollhouse cookies or angel-food cake? Throughout the ages the preparation of food and sharing of meals have formed some of our most vivid personal and family memories.

There was a time, however, when the kitchen was not even part of the house as we know it. In the seventeenth and eighteenth centuries, the homes of the prosperous middle classes had no specifically designated dining area and the kitchen facilities were detached from the main house. Because stoves and ovens were crude contraptions in which to contain burning logs, the threat of fire to the basically flammable house encouraged architects to remove the kitchen facilities as far as possible from the family residence. In an age when the privileged classes employed armies of servants to prepare and serve meals and clean up afterward, the kitchens were usually out of sight.

The kitchens of the olden days did not have hot running water, gas flames at the flick of a knob, electrical ventilation systems to remove unwanted odors, or garbage disposals to whisk away leftover food. And without reliable refrigeration systems, most food, if not promptly cooked and eaten, spoiled rapidly. Let's face it, cooking a meal without the modern appliances we have today was a dreadful, time-consuming chore.

Of course, although the lower classes were not spared the unpleasant aspects of cooking, they did derive a pleasure that the more affluent families were denied: the joy of clustering around the family hearth, helping to peel vegetables, stirring stews, smelling the delicious aromas, while trading stories. In short, the homes of peasants, workers, farmers, and laborers always contained a room that has since evolved into our modern, idealized kitchen—a relaxed, yet busy family room that serves as the strategic and emotional center of the home and family.

Today, the average home design incorporates the three basic mealtime activities—preparing and serving food, dining, and cleaning up—in one vicinity or two conveniently adjacent areas. This kitchen space has become, and probably will remain, a psychological focal point of family life as well as a physical one. Here are the childhood memories of enormous meals mysteriously prepared by grownups who, alone, could master the formidable and often forbidden appliances with their dangers and delights. Here is where you gathered with your teenage friends, snacking and talking of your future hopes and dreams late into the night. The kitchen is where you shared many of the happiest moments early in your marriage, when your own children were young. And in later years, it is still around the kitchen table with a cup of coffee or tea in hand that

Here is a simple kitchen corner that radiates a soft warmth with blue-gray cabinetry surrounded by white ceiling, floor, and French doors. A darker blue highlights the cookery and the cabinet handles. The room is also unified by the designer's decision to use only square and rectangular shapes, unlike the previous kitchen where concave and convex surfaces created an undulating effect. In a room such as this, where one tone predominates, the overall effect is not blunted by accessories or decorative touches that would upset the chromatic balance. Here, dried flowers, an old tin, and two antique bottles sit atop the cabinets, and a ceramic duck and canisters find their own nook lower, blending into the misty hue of the room.

The sculpture of a nineteenth-century maid sitting on the modern countertop sets the tone for this converted butler's pantry turned twentieth-century kitchen. When the owners of this nearly one-hundred-year-old country mansion on Long Island refinished this area, they decided to leave the revolving service window in the center of the pickled oak buffet. The window was originally built to prevent foul cooking odors from escaping into the dining room and spoiling the meal. Note the painting on the wall that depicts the matching floor and ceiling done in vanilla and chocolate colors. If you look closely enough, you'll be surprised to see that the painting is accurate even down to including a painting of the painting.

you reminisce about times past. For the kitchen has always been a nurturing room, a room for sharing and companionship. In fact, in Latin the word companion means "with bread." A true companion is someone with whom we will break and share bread, someone we will invite to join us in the private and intimate world of a family meal.

To enrich this companionship and intimacy, the kitchen should be a warm bright room, both physically and emotionally. If the kitchen has a sunny southern exposure, the sun is more than a frequent guest; it is also a provider of light and heat. A kitchen with large open windows is a joy to be in. However, few kitchens can afford to sacrifice precious wall space for windows because the kitchen, of every room in the house, requires the greatest lengths of wall for the large appliances and the many cabinets needed for storage. A skylight in the kitchen is the perfect solution if you want bright natural light.

In any event, the best kitchens are those with adjustable light to accommodate different needs: high bright light to prevent eyestrain, targeted specifically at work areas so you can see clearly how much spice you are adding; subdued dreamy light to embellish a romantic meal for two; strong general light for cleaning up after a meal, washing dishes, or sweeping up crumbs; and steady even light for doing homework at the kitchen table. Most important is the light that can illuminate the specific area in which you are working or sitting. No one enjoys eating a meal in one's own shadow, nor is it easy to prepare a meal in the dark. A series of track lights properly arranged and aimed will provide light when and where you need it you need it and will allow you to turn

This is another kitchen developed from a converted butler's pantry. In this one, the original roof structure was retained to add a coarser element to this otherwise smoothly finished room. In olden days, many houses employed this curved ribbed design to lend strength to the ceiling. Now this heavy-looking brick ceiling accents the delicate Picasso vases used as decorative touches above the cabinets. Incandescent lighting under the cabinetry is pleasantly balanced by overhead ceiling lights, so the charm of the old-style ceiling is not lost when the work areas are illuminated. There is an extra storage drawer recessed in the toe-space under the lower cabinets beneath the range, an ideal spot for storing bulky pots and pans.

This unusual space is highly unified by the generous use of rich, dark woods—in the floor, the work island, the cabinets, and the arched door and doorway. A raised nook on the far left houses a potbellied stove. The curved and arched woodwork of the cabinet doors, the main door, and even the end panels of the work island is masterfully done; the end effect is a kitchen that suggests high-quality values both in decor and nutrition. This is a healthy-looking room, committed to elegant but comfortable standards—a kitchen solidly designed and appointed for cooking meals to be prepared and enjoyed.

off lighting in the areas not in use.

The most inviting kitchens smell wonderful, and the art of producing those delicious aromas includes eliminating unpleasant smells as much as it does the culinary skill needed to create mouth-watering ones. Fresh air scented with the enticing aroma of cooking food means fresh air free of greasy fumes, stale food odors, moisture, and steam. When the weather is cooperative, windows can be opened to provide fresh air and remove stale odors. However, during the winter or in a kitchen without windows, unpleasant odors will need to be eliminated by using vents and exhaust ducts. Without proper ventilation, some of the major pleasures of kitchen life will never be enjoyed—the smell of fresh cookies still warm on the cookie sheet, the aroma of chili cooking on Saturday afternoon, or the scent of a Sunday roast baking slowly in the oven.

The kitchen is one of the most heavily trafficked rooms in the house, and the arrangement of doors always determines the traffic flow. Like windows, doors create dead space as far as kitchen appliances are concerned, and yet most traditional kitchens have at least two doorways, one exiting out of the house or onto the back porch, the other leading into the dining area or another room of the house. But those aren't the only ones! A kitchen is a beehive of doors, opening, closing, slamming, swinging into each other, waiting to bump your head or bang your knee. Cabinets and shelves with sliding doors can eliminate much of the nuisance.

The appliances in most kitchens can be arranged in one of three basic patterns: U-shaped, L-shaped, or straight line, depending on how many walls

The designers of this kitchen successfully and ingeniously utilized the major wall space for cabinetry, and they created substantial storage areas under the spacious countertops. All front elements are composed of fully rounded horizontal lines and coated with a durable, easily washable seamless material. The lipped handles on all doors and drawers are unobtrusive, both visually and physically. The profusion of horizontals, covering most wall space, in this kitchen gives it its unique character and eliminates the need for extensive decoration. Care was taken to temper the horizontal and ribbed look by contrasting it with the simple white square tiles used on the floor, the work counters, and the backsplash.

A judicious use of color and pattern achieve the dignified quality of this well-balanced kitchen. The solid beige squares on the floor and walls match the rectangular surfaces of the cabinets and appliances. The rust red ceiling, however, is characterised by thinly drawn lines of interlocking squares, creating an effect of lightness above while the bulk and weight remain below. Also consider how much of the overall effect is determined by the decision to extend the floor pattern over the sink and move the ceiling pattern down the walls to the top of the cabinets—a room that begins above and below and meets somewhere halfway between in one's imagination.

This blue-and-white kitchen looks like a charmingly fun arboretum of light and greenery. The trellis motif separates the actual kitchen area from the garden supply room which, because of the wall-size mirror behind it, looks like a much larger section of the kitchen than it actually is. Plain white pots, both those containing plants and those being held in reserve, contribute to the garden motif. And of course, any devoted gardener would have bouquets of fresh-cut flowers to lend color and fragrance to the eating and cooking areas. Surprisingly, the room is not cluttered with greenery. A few wisely placed plants and the magic of mirrors produce the playfully cluttered effect while most of the room is actually clear to function as a real kitchen.

The disco look of this kitchen suggests that it belongs to someone who loves midnight adventures—and it does. The bachelor who lives here asserts that it is the ultimate "kitchen for now." The mood is late night, the feel is sensuous—even when the sun still shines outside. Marzzi tile covers the floor, the counters, and backsplashes, with laminated edges running the length of the wraparound counter that turns determinedly almost full circle. Brass tamber cabinets ripple with light that shines through the similarly ribbed light fixtures overhead. A "hot" kitchen, it even incorporates instant hot water at the turn of the tap, a sensible feature for areas where water shortages are a regular problem.

A decision every homeowner must make is whether each room will have its own unique look or whether an overall design concept will be used throughout the house. These people opted for the latter and created a stately kitchen that is wonderfully joined to nearby rooms. The magnificently paneled hardwood floor extends out to the sunken living room, and the mauve-brown cabinetry complements other muted colors used in the living room and the room beyond the sink. The end cabinet on the left is, in fact, the partition that separates, and yet joins, two distinct areas. The twelve-sided work island in the middle perfectly fits this kitchen, which seems to radiate out to all other sections of the house.

are utilized for the major appliances and work areas. Each kitchen, whether large or small, is tailored to the space into which it must fit. An important guideline in design, applicable to all shapes, is that the fewer steps it takes to prepare, serve, and clean up after a meal, the better. No one wants to walk themselves to death preparing Chicken Marengo! In the course of a year, managing a poorly laid-out kitchen can require literally hundreds of miles of needless walking.

Like everything in the kitchen, the floor demands one all-important feature: it must be easy to clean. Families don't just eat in kitchens; they *live* in them, and no family can really live in a kitchen without getting the floor dirty. There is no such thing as an "occasional spill"; spills are eternal. Crumbs, footprints, snow-encrusted boots that leave chunks of dirty ice behind them, even the innocent kitten dribbling milk as she scampers off to her less-than-innocent pastimes will leave the kitchen floor looking, at the end of the day, as if you had not really cleaned it up the night before. Hard floor materials such as tile or terrazzo are easy to clean but hard to walk on. Soft indoor-outdoor carpeting is gentler on the feet, but no matter what the advertisements tell you, spills are always messy and a nuisance to shampoo out. Cushioned vinyl has become the favorite alternative; it is padded enough to make the long hours on your feet less fatiguing, and its surface is hard enough to make cleaning up relatively easy. Wise home decorators choose a pattern and color that, besides complementing the overall design of the room, will hide of dirt, stains, and "occasional spills."

Basic colors for the kitchen walls have traditionally been warm ones that suggest homeyness, or bright ones to indicate cleanliness. Because the kitchen can become rather warm when ovens are on and pots are boiling on the stove, reds and oranges only intensify the suggestion of heat. An extremely bright and hot color can become garish and psychologically unpleasant if there is no way to temper it with softer lights or alternative color patterns for contrast. Light and color must be flexible. Not every meal should be eaten in a spotlight of bright color. If the kitchen is particularly small, cool receding colors such as light greens and blues will create the illusion of more space. Northern kitchens and those shaded from sunlight can stand brighter colors on the walls and floors, but there should be areas of deep, rich color, such as in permanent fixtures, for contrast. Remember that the kitchen is used almost every hour of the day, and the nighttime hours as well. Select colors and wall patterns that can change with the time, mood, and occasion.

*A*s you roam in and out of the kitchens in this book you'll sense the family character of each, for the kitchen is truly a family room. It attracts every member of the household naturally and effortlessly. Some kitchens we have selected reflect the warm friendliness of the families who use them. Others suggest the formal setting enjoyed by families or couples whose aim is to cater to guests and outsiders rather than to the needs of family members. Some are practical, some impractical. Many traditional kitchens look as if they are eternal, stable, and have been bequeathed to the present occupants by older generations. Other kitchens look as though they may be out of fashion tomorrow.

This small galley kitchen looks larger than it is because of the wizardry wrought by the opaqued glass doors on the cabinets. Solid cabinet doors would have created a heavy "walled" effect, making the space feel narrow and more cramped than it is. Clear glass panes would have made the area look cluttered, with dishes and accessories in plain view. The ghostly forms behind the fogged panels, however, merely suggest themselves and do not intrude. At the same time, the cabinets themselves seem to hover over the sink and large appliances. Once the illusion of space was achieved, the owner felt unabashed at adding a magnificent hood over the range. Although it looks antique, it is a new vent aged to look as if it survived from an earlier day.

For a long time, stainless steel has been used in kitchen appliances, and today the stainless steel look even dominates the color and texture of some kitchens. The silvery gray of steel is seen on the cabinetry in this kitchen. The floor tiles, too, match the tones, and of course, the sinks and the pots hanging on the walls need not apologize for being too utilitarian. The careful decoration of this kitchen offsets whatever cold effect stainless steel and gray might produce; note the use of soft rose light over the main sink and off-white paint on the walls. The hardwood counter around the wet bar mollifies the room, as does the deeply recessed ceiling painted a dark comforting hue.

Indeed, many people redecorate kitchens almost as frequently as they redo other rooms.

However it is laid out, no matter how the appliances are arranged, whatever the color schemes and the knick-knacks and the patterns on the wall, the kitchen will always be a room of many purposes: working, resting, eating, cleaning up, relaxing, reflecting. The kitchen witnesses family camaraderie and family crises. It accommodates the constant flow of people, whether they be the immediate family, neighbors, friends, delivery men, the pets, or you alone during a moment of solitude . . . for everyone moves into and beyond the kitchen. In spite of the commotion, the kitchen is a room of welcome, nourishment, and good cheer, a room that reflects the seasons of your life as well as the seasons of the year. More than in any other room, the time of year can be surmised from what is going on in the kitchen, what's cooking, and—say!—what smells so good? All of these things—the hot soups and stews of winter; the lure of freshly perked coffee on cold mornings; the return of fresh fruit and berries; the clink of ice cubes in tall cold drinks on hot summer days; the picnic and barbeque "fixins' " laid out and waiting to be packed; the sweet pungent smell of cider in the autumn; the boiling preserves that will be canned and enjoyed in the cold months to come—are the special things that create a true kitchen all year 'round.

As you wander through the kitchens we have mapped out for you, you will see all this and more, for no one ever enters a kitchen to remember it simply in terms of walls, appliances, floors, cupboards, and windows. The kitchen has always been much more than that. It has been our favorite people, the best of times, hearty meals, a deep sense of security and happiness—a place where everyone has felt at home, a place to belong.

Here is a room that carries the stainless steel motif to its ultimate conclusion! Rather than just using the metal as a suggestion here and there, the designer who owns this kitchen chose to extend the material right up the walls and onto the ceiling. The sloped ceiling makes this galley kitchen look as if it might indeed be in the hull of a ship. The solid monochromatic heaviness of the room is tempered by the aquamarine mosaic tiles on the floor and the bright orange acrylic sink. A kitchen like this, without windows for natural ventilation, needs easily washable material—like steel—throughout, so grease buildup and condensation can be removed from the low ceiling and close walls.

"Slim and trim" is the phrase for this kitchen—stainless steel countertop, polished granite on floor and window ledges, the smooth unadorned wood on walls and ceiling. All are mysteriously highlighted by the dark glass windows. When all the accessories are put away, as they are in this photograph, the room takes on an eerie quality of meticulous efficiency in a setting of sylvan spontaneity. This long narrow space, lined with large windows that protect it from the less controlled elements outside, is just the kitchen for a cook who wants the hours spent in preparing food to be a time encapsulated from outside distractions, yet needs the inspiration of natural beauty to enhance the culinary craft.

For many people, the joy of living in a loft is to let the origins of the space dominate the decor. This New York apartment retains the pressed tin ceiling and rough-hewn beams and pillars that support the building. The kitchen has been deliberately zoned off from the living room by the long counter that contains a sink, work space, and dining area. Industrial elements are conspicuous in the stove, the warehouse light fixtures, and the exposed pipes. The entire loft, however, is unified by the long rows of ceramic floor tiles that alternate off-white and soft gray. The total achievement here is the pleasing balance of sleek modern features with older textures and structures.

The parquet floor in this kitchen is just one of the extra touches the owners made to transform this kitchen into a room of outstanding elegance. Deciding on wood as the primary material, they chose traditional cabinetry accompanied by unique features such as ample pigeonholes and convenient pull-down fruit and vegetable larders. To save space a retractable table slides easily under the counter. Pulled out, it more than doubles the available work space in the area.

A hardy pioneer spirit is evoked in this kitchen, designed to create the rough, unpolished look of an early settler's cabin. Located appropriately in North Carolina, the simple wood room is "complete" but has an "unfinished" look. Without ceiling boards, the wooden joists supporting the second floor are clearly visible. Nailheads in the cabinets contribute to the primitive motif, as does the curtainless window. Lighting is provided by traditionally shaped light bulbs; even the wiring remains in view. Countertops are laminated with dark chocolate brown to add contrast to the light pine wood without detracting from the basic material. Wicker chairs that creak when you sit in them provide the perfect touch for this room of beams, joists, and panels.

Many families favor a kitchen in which not every wall is a wall. Since adjoining rooms, such as dining rooms, family rooms, and breakfast nooks, are often used in conjunction with kitchen activities, it makes sense not to seal them off from each other by solid walls. The result is the half wall or serving counter. But here that basic idea is presented with a delightful and practical twist. Rather than losing useful storage space, this designer chose to continue the row of cabinets across the half wall both above and below the serving counter. To provide lightness and openness, the upper cabinets have glass doors on both sides so you can see through them and so accessories stored here can be reached from either side.

Family life today is characterized by togetherness and openness, and this is reflected in the way space is created and defined. Using the concept that major family activities can and should take place in one setting, this house contains only the faintest suggestion that it is made up of individual rooms. A handsome divider partitions one side of the living room; on the other side is the dining room, to which the kitchen in the far background is visually attached by the use of similar materials and colors in its cabinets.

The white walls and ceiling in this home draw all three rooms together, the distinct areas being delineated only by such features as rugs in the dining and living sections and the traditional kitchen flooring.

When converting an older house into a contemporary home for modern living, you can harmonize touches of the past with premonitions of things to come. This family successfully blended the past and the future in their kitchen of white lacquer and oak-plank flooring by retaining the original style windows and cabinetry as a sleek modern range module serves as a room divider and work counter. As in olden days when the kitchen was the physical hub of the home, this kitchen still draws people with its open and inviting wholesomeness. This is the perfect kitchen for the cook who enjoys seeing others and chatting with them while preparing meals.

A peculiar wall that juts into a kitchen need not become an obstacle to efficient kitchen layout. In this case, the L-shaped space that this homeowner had to work with was cleverly utilized for both storage and work. On the left, within easy reach from the eating area is the dishware, silver, and bowls of fruit. Clear glass door panels let the carefully arranged stacks of plates, bowls, saucers, and hanging cups become part of the decor. On the right are closed cabinets containing less decorative cookware and small appliances along with a work counter close to the stove, refrigerator, and sink. This kitchen is really livable and workable, not one that is to be admired but never disturbed. Even the busy zigzag pattern in the wall tiles echoes the energy that gives this kitchen its distinctive charm.

Take every advantage of window space when laying out work areas. Even though much kitchen work is "heads down" activity, proper lighting and the opportunity for occasional glances up and out can turn kitchen chores into tasks that nourish the creative spirit. Here is a work counter ideally set up for preparing homemade breads. A marble top is best for rolling, kneading, and shaping dough. The gift of natural light cannot be beat, and these windows allow generous amounts to enter. Still, they provide privacy from neighbors—who might be inclined to drop by just a little too often when they see fresh bread cooling by the window.

This upstairs kitchen and dining room are built immediately under the rafters of a cinder block home in England. But the architect who designed and owns this house managed to pull light in from the second-story patio by using a glass door and installing a floor-to-ceiling window, eliminating the solid wall that would have kept this galley work area in the dark. Additional light enters through the service window between the kitchen and the eating area in the far back. The quarry tile floor, exposed rafters, unfinished wood, and cinder block walls render a simplicity and primitive naturalness to this private home.

Californians are famous for grabbing every ray of sunlight they can. This West Coast architect ingeniously designed his own home to allow the maximum amount of light to enter. The magnificent window and skylight that seems to crawl up the wall of this kitchen provides a breathtaking expanse that lets the spirits soar even when the hands are doing the most down-to-earth chores over the sink or range. The concept employed here could be used in any home when the eye-level view outdoors leaves much to be desired, but the space overhead opens onto trees and sky. Simply use the wall space for necessary appliances and create a view through the ceiling and upper wall.

Here is another solution to the problem of inadequate light in a kitchen when either the view outside is unattractive or the cook wants privacy from neighbors and passers-by. A wall of solid glass brick lets sunlight enter along with a flicker of color and movement when activity occurs outside. An added incentive for using glass bricks over the stove area is that the bricks can take the heat and are easy to wipe clean of condensation, steam, or greasy buildup. They also solve the problem of how to trim a kitchen window when it would be dangerous to have curtains so close to the range.

Often the outdoor entrance to the kitchen is neglected, but the designer of this home saw an opportunity to enhance the total aesthetic impact of the kitchen. This view perfectly balances line, shape, and color. The glass overhang parallels the angle of the interior stairway. The sleek curvature of the oblong work island is echoed in the hemispheric light fixtures on either side of the entrance. Even the color scheme is superbly matched, with black accenting the French doors, handrail, overhang, and flower box, and earth tones dominating the exterior brick as well as the woodwork indoors.

Here's a clear indication that simplicity is often utterly engaging. A humble saltbox of a house shouldn't try to ape the opulence of a luxury home. The plain painted wood on the walls and ceiling of this kitchen has a nobility of its own, especially when left unadorned. The cottage-style windows give this room a bright airiness, and their panes echo the pattern of the traditional black-and-white checkerboard floor. Two materials divide this long work counter: the highly sealed and polished wood around the sink and the granite-textured acrylic top in the corner. A fortunate cook, indeed, can work in this clear serviceable kitchen surrounded by honest natural light.

*Color, shape, and light work in perfect harmony in this large, roomy kitchen.
Indirect lighting steps down, platform by platform, over the range and work island.
Concentrated beams shine from the bottom of the upper cabinets, perfectly
illuminating the countertops. Large four-sided panels determine the lines of the
room in a series of squares like the wooden lattice that drops from the ceiling. A
mysterious touch of depth is created by the mirrored siding under the range.*

Many good-looking kitchens capture our admiration by the simplicity with which their materials are arranged. In this one, all the appliances and fittings are wood and stainless steel in a room of bright walls and spacious windows. Shelves, cabinetry, and floor are of varied wood textures, while sinks, range areas, and countertops exhibit the muted shine of metal. The unusual lighting fixture overhead is a fascinating metal sculpture in its own right and allows centers of light to be aimed strategically at important work areas or to be bounced off the ceiling for more uniform illumination. The windows have been kept bare of curtains or blinds to let the cook, through most of the day, work in the bright atmosphere of natural, sunshiny light.

Like the kitchen to the left, this one achieves its overall effect by line and light. Whereas the other room retained a soft uniform lighting throughout to match the coloring, this kitchen startles the imagination by juxtaposing unexpected lighting effects and nonsymmetrical shapes. The ceiling, cracked by strident yellow lighting, is made up of various geometrical shapes and levels, characterized by sharp angular cuts in dark wood panels. Beneath it the room is lit with natural light, and the beige cabinetry—more predictable in its traditional design—is a pleasant contrast. The small alcove on the left glows with a phosphorescence, highlighting the midnight blue tiles for yet another light and color option.

2

Permanent Fixtures

Appliances can make a kitchen, and here the black front panels of the major appliances contrast beautifully with the wood tone in which they are set. The two-door refrigerator on the left and the microwave and conventional ovens on the right are situated to save steps when moving from one to the other. The cook range on the island is close to the refrigerator and the main sink, with the main dishwasher underneath the sink. Cooking in this kitchen is especially enjoyable because of its sensible layout. A smaller sink and dishwasher on the center island are ideal for cleaning up after light meals because they are close to the eating area and the diminutive dishwasher saves water and energy. The bold black-paneled appliances are nicely complemented by black accents such as the trim on the pot and pan rack overhead and on the clock.

There are three essential features in any kitchen: the stove, the refrigerator, and the sink—usually sharing space with an assortment of cabinets, cupboards, and flat work surfaces. How these fixtures are arranged can make or break a kitchen. The most efficient kitchens are designed so that a minimum of steps is required to move from area to area in the course of preparing a meal. Saving steps by having necessary food and equipment at your fingertips or within arm's reach can transform cooking a meal from drudgery into delightful creativity. Therefore, the arrangement of the four key areas—storage, preparation, dining, and clean-up—determine the ease and grace with which a chef can turn out meals, serve them, and remove dishes and leftovers when the meal has ended. When these areas are located in a logical progression from one to the next, and the doorways are situated so that the flow of kids, pets, and neighbors through the kitchen is not directly across the work axis, getting a meal together, whether it be soup and a sandwich or an eight-course dinner, can be fun and enjoyable.

*E*very meal begins and ends at the sink—washing hands before handling food, rinsing vegetables and meats before cooking them, washing dishes, and finally, washing hands again to remove the smell of greasy water and detergent. In the course of preparing a meal, hygienic cooks rinse their hands several times as they move from one task to another. It is, therefore, crucial that the sink be centrally located for all of these trips, ideally between the stove and the refrigerator. As many kids have pointed out, the most boring and the cruellest task of all, bordering on slave labor, is washing dishes after a

meal. Such being the case, it has become traditional for interior designers to place the sink under a window to relieve the boredom and provide light and fresh air. Because washing dishes doesn't require intense concentration, the view from the window can be a welcome relief to the task at hand.

It was once a mark of status, but is now a learned necessity, for families to have dishwashers—electric rather than human. In the past you had to scrape and rinse the dirty dishes so thoroughly before placing them in the dishwasher that you might just as well have spent a few extra minutes and done the whole job yourself. Today's dishwashers perform more efficiently, but it is still questionable whether a single person or a couple need to suffer the expense, the noise, and the aggravation for so few dishes. Yet, in one respect, the electric dishwasher has proven a godsend—it often eliminates the nightly squabble over who is going to do the dishes.

*H*ave you ever been a weekend guest and offered to cook breakfast only to notice (how had you overlooked it when you made the offer!?) that your hosts cook with electricity and you only know the perfect temperature to cook omelettes on gas? The long-running controversy over whether gas or electricity is easier to cook with will never be settled. There are numerous factors complicating the argument, such as whether the gas will leak in the kitchen if someone is not careful or whether a formal dinner party will be ruined when there is a power failure in the neighborhood. As far as the cost of each goes, well, they always go up! So the decision between an electric or a gas stove is each his or her own.

The best place for a stove is some-

where other than near a doorway or a window, where sudden gusts of wind can blow out the gas flames or where curtains can be blown into the flame and catch fire. Also, the heat generated from the stove will steam up windows and cause them to get greasier faster, so it is advisable to place the stove on the other side of the room.

Stoves themselves will be troublesome in one fashion or another until manufacturers design the perfect one. Consider a fundamental problem: where to place the controls. Should they be placed on the front where children can play with them and party guests lean against them? Or should they be placed on top in the back where long flouncy sleeves must be dragged across the cookware and the flames to reach the controls? Perhaps all these questions will become obsolete as the kitchen of the future becomes a totally microwave environment. We're thinking of a future far removed from the current controversy over whether food tastes better cooked in a radar range, or over gas flames, electric heat, or old-fashioned fire! Can *you* tell the difference?

*H*istorically, people did ingenious things to keep food from spoiling: "Eating it fast" has always been the most satisfying and safest method, but not necessarily the most practical. Fruit cellars were created to preserve many perishables. Burying the perishables in the ground in winter was another option, but this strategy worked only in northern climates. Centuries ago humans discovered that certain spices pounded into meats would preserve them and cover up the foul smell and taste produced if you kept them for very long, but you always took your chances that they had spoiled. In

The design options displayed in this kitchen include a magnificent industrial stove which surprisingly doesn't seem out of place in a room whose robin's-egg blue and eggshell white coloring give the whole space a delicate, feathery weightlessness. Observe how naturally the size and bulk of a stainless-steel commercial stove fits right in, suggesting that the sheer bulk of large appliances need not limit the design concepts used. The large burgundy-and-white enclosure for the range hood matches the red details on the stove, and its own size counterbalances that of the stove. So which weighs more, a pound of metal or a pound of feathers? In this kitchen they obviously weigh the same and both have a right to be there.

These latest models in hobs and cooking zones are just a few of the many styles created in recent years that let the kitchen designer choose combinations to meet individual needs. In the center is a cooktop that includes an electric barbecue grill on the left, two-ring electric hobs in the middle, and a hob encased in a slim ceramic panel on the right, which can serve as a braising area or can be adjusted to function as a complete cooking area. Together the three areas form a single well-planned unit that is attractive and efficient. On the upper right is a combination gas range, electric hob, and deep-fryer, stylishly modern and designed for easy cleaning. The hob panel on the lower right incorporates the latest technology that heats up the hot plates fast and efficiently. Each cook ring is housed in an insulating material that directs heat upward, thus saving energy.

Here is a built-in double oven, totally electric. The lower is a traditional oven; the upper is equipped with a fan duct. Electronic digital clocks can program the main oven for as much as six hours of cooking, up to twenty-four hours in advance. Both sections have see-through double-glazed doors. Additional features include separate, removable grill and rotisserie elements, interior lights so you can see how your meal is coming along, and removable liner panels on the main oven for easy washing. The sleek, modern look of this appliance is echoed throughout the kitchen in the oblong knobs of the cabinets and the chain link wallpaper.

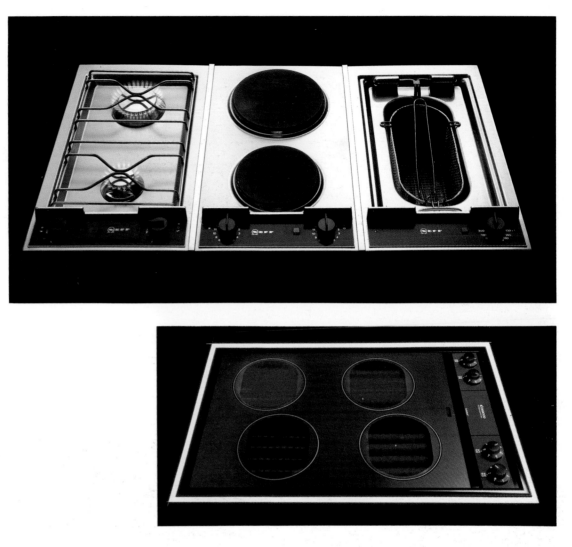

villages and large cities that had self-contained, convenient neighborhoods, people shopped every day for perishables and were able to keep them overnight on a large block of ice housed in a wooden container; this became known as the "ice box." And so refrigerators had their crude beginnings.

Today's refrigerators come in an array of styles with many options: two doors, one door, vertical doors next to each other, horizontal doors one above the other. The most important consideration for the door of a refrigerator is the direction in which it swings. There

are right-handed and left-handed refrigerators; the efficient kitchen layout will use the one that makes the most sense in terms of the direction from which the "fridge" is approached most often. If you must always walk around the open door to the other side, it adds steps and often keeps the door open longer than necessary. You'll most appreciate the direction the door swings when it comes time to defrost the freezer. The old-fashioned technique (still required by some of the most modern freezers!) requires carrying pans of boiling water from the stove to the fridge, replacing them

as they cool and intercepting mammoth chunks of ice that fall from the sides of the refrigerator. And keep in mind that even with steady nerves it is not possible to carry a full defrost tray from the fridge to the sink without creating small tidal waves that splash onto the floor. It is important to have as short a distance as possible to go, with few twists and turns on the way. As with stoves, perhaps in the not-too-distant future, manufacturers will engineer a more perfect refrigerator, but don't get your hopes up. Look how long it took them to realize that a refrigerator on rollers is easier to move

A different view of the kitchen displayed on page 35 uncovers another unusual feature—a commercial refrigerator with four glass doors and interior lighting that can be turned on while the doors are closed. Unlike the average domestic fridge, you don't have to open the door to discover what's in it or—more likely than not—what's been eaten. The interior is painted blue to harmonize with the dominant color in the room, and the four sections echo the large check pattern of the wallpaper.

out from the wall in order to clean behind it. Rollers! Why didn't anyone think of that earlier?

*N*o matter how technologically advanced your appliances are, preparing meals is no fun without plenty of work surface. When all is said and done it is still human ability, not machinery, that turns out the great meals: chopping, kneading, stirring, mincing, peeling, slicing, and so forth must be done by you. Ingredients need to wait their turn to be added, they need to be at your fingertips, and they need to be in sight so you remember whether you added them yet. It sounds simple and basic, and it is, but a kitchen that has not been designed to offer the cook an assortment of counters and work areas is a kitchen that violates an important ingredient in preparing any meal— enjoyment. And enjoyment comes from the ease with which a job can be done. When designing your kitchen, arrange work surfaces at the proper height so that they are comfortable for the people who will actually be using them. Because most cooking tasks keep you on your feet, include at least one counter where you can sit and work. Traditional work surfaces are wood (great for cutting and chopping), marble (wonderful for laying out pastry and dough), and tile (especially near the stove for receiving hot items). The newer materials, such as formica and plastic laminates, need special care because knives can scratch them and harsh chemicals may leave nasty stains or ruin the surfaces.

The refrigerators in these two kitchens show how wooden paneling on the doors can be used to tie the appliances to the dominant wood texture. On the left, the light blond laminated wood used as trim on the shelves and countertops also serves as the material for the room divider. When applied to the refrigerator too, an occasional element in the kitchen becomes a dominant design factor. This is an ideal way to incorporate wood textures when you don't want a completely wood-paneled kitchen. The kitchen on the lower right, however, is predominantly wood—cabinetry, door, and molding. Even the rich floor tiles and wallpaper near the ceiling echo the colors and grains of wood. In this case, the wood-paneled refrigerator becomes a necessity for the obvious warmth the designer intended for this room. So whether you need just touches of wood or whether wood is your primary material, the large surfaces of the refrigerator can complement your decor.

*I*t seems to be a kind of Murphy's Law of Kitchens that there are never enough cupboards. But often this is a human problem rather than a physical one. Kitchen people are notorious pack rats; they save everything. Often the solution is not to add more cupboards or cabinets but to start throwing things out. Kitchens that are easy to work in also have a clear and logical system for storage. Items are grouped by type (such as food, cookware, dishware, cutlery, linens, cleaning materials, and so forth) and then stored according to whether they are used often or seldom. Another guideline is to store items close to the area where they will be needed in order to cut down the distance required to step, stoop, and stretch. Cooking a meal should *not* be an aerobic activity. Many cabinets and shelves have considerable "dead space" in them, either behind shelved items or over them, when the shelves are too far apart or of an improper depth. It takes a bit of ingenuity to organize the storage areas of the kitchen properly, but it also requires a good memory to remember what is hidden where...and of course, what you've thrown out!

*T*he large permanent fixtures in the kitchen are indeed large and in most cases permanent. This suggests that they be selected and purchased carefully. For example, the color of these appliances will determine color and decorating schemes for some time to come. The wrong color can limit your options for future redecorating plans.

When one fixture needs to be replaced, you may discover that you can't get the exact color match. And repairs of a too complicated appliance can also be costly and ongoing. Remember, enough can go wrong in a kitchen in the first place. The simpler and more basic the equipment, the smaller the chance of repairs and costly maintenance charges. In the showrooms, the latest technological wizardry can be mesmerizing. At home it can be downright aggravating, especially when you realize that the extra added conveniences really only mean extra commissions for the sales personnel...people who will never cook in your kitchen!

Traditionally, sinks were the most unexciting and unappealing element in the kitchen—a place where dirty, greasy dishes and cookware collected; where the primary job was distasteful, hot, and messy; and where aesthetic charm was generally missing. In recent years, however, manufacturers have remedied the last complaint, offering homeowners a large selection of shapes, colors, styles, and materials. The sinks shown here are just two possibilities. On the right is a one-and-a-half bowl combination, made of matte black enamel. It comes with a matching drain rack and a cutting board cover for the smaller bowl. Enamel sinks today are more chip-resistant and are able to withstand harsh chemicals.

On the left is a small sink for preparing food, rinsing vegetables, and washing hands. The advantage of a small food-preparation sink is that it provides a place to rinse food when the main sink is cluttered with dirty dishes. It is more hygienic; you know fresh vegetables and fruit can drain free from grease or suds.

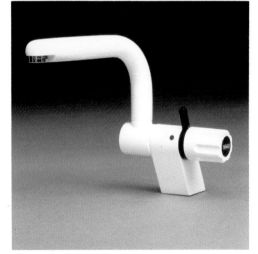

Beauty and utility are joined in both of these modern tap models. Each incorporates the arched lift faucet that is a must for rinsing large pots and pans. The faucet on the left is made of white acrylic and similar styles are available in a wide range of color combinations to match the decor of almost any kitchen. Its nonswivel spout is perfect for single-bowl sinks. The one on the right is stainless steel and the handles are tilted toward the user, a sensible touch for ease of operation.

So often the do-it-yourself home designer believes that for the components of a kitchen to harmonize they must match in an almost unobtrusive manner. Yet obtrusiveness becomes a virtue in this kitchen by the bold choice of a shiny stainless-steel dishwasher in a line of somber cabinetry. With subtle touches, such as the cabinet handles and faucet as well as the edging on the dishwasher, this heavy-duty appliance becomes an integral part of the room. For another angle on this interesting kitchen, see p. 118.

The cluttered charm of this kitchen is not solely a designer's whim; it is a necessity. Look closely and you'll see that this space is only as wide as a very narrow stove. In a wraparound environment like this, everything is at your fingertips simply because it has nowhere else to go! And yet the usefulness of the extra sink in the foreground for washing and rinsing produce makes this cozy corner a two-sink kitchen. Because of the parallel work surfaces made of wood, a cook in this room will have an easier time preparing meals than in a more spacious kitchen with many steps between inconveniently placed work counters. The many bright copper surfaces here enhance the warmth and specialness of this kitchen as they catch the last rays of the late afternoon sun.

Most modern homes do not have dusty wine cellars to conjure up the romance of patiently aged bottles lying on their sides, waiting to be selected for that special occasion. In fact, many homeowners never consider wine storage when they purchase kitchen appliances. That's not the case with this wine connoisseur! Here is a wine cooler that will keep a large supply of bottles at a constant temperature, to prevent them from maturing too rapidly. Ideally located in the dining area, this wine "cellar" offers easy accessibility. Here, wines that are not to be opened for several weeks can be placed horizontally, so the corks do not dry out and shrink, which would then allow air to enter the bottles and cause the wine to sour.

3

Accessories

"A place for everything, and everything in its place." When stated about a kitchen, this old aphorism can conjure up headaches. Probably no other room in the house collects as much "stuff" as does the kitchen, and in no other room is there the constant hustle and bustle that requires that all the utensils and odds-and-ends be easily managed. Storage is a primary factor in a successfully organized kitchen, and the most effective are the ones, like this one, that achieve a degree of aesthetic attractiveness in their practicality and efficiency—everything within easy reach. This designer not only welcomes the "well-stocked" look but exaggerates it by installing mirrors behind the shelving to create the illusion that there are twice as many things—but not twice as many shelves!

The kitchen is a collection of odd items: large and small, old and new, practical and whimsical, some safe and others dangerous, some used constantly and others very seldom. In traditional farmhouse kitchens, there seemed to be little inclination to put away the equipment used for preparing food, possibly because the farmhouse kitchen was the archetypal kitchen, used by the families who produced the food the rest of the nation ate. They were people who understood food and nutrition, worked hard and long from sunrise to sunset, and needed nourishing, stick-to-the-ribs meals—hearty meals for hearty lives. For people whose lives were centered around the growing, processing, and handling of food there was little need to remove kitchen accessories; most were left out on open shelves or partially concealed behind the glass doors of cabinets and cupboards. And indeed, the knives, canisters, jars, bowls, baskets, towels, pots, pans, yes, even plates, were seldom empty and unused. Food preparation was a naturally full-time job.

*E*ven the accessories themselves were made of natural materials such as wood, metal, cloth, pottery, glass. These utensils were made by and for the hand—objects that retained the comforting smells and stains of delicious and memorable food and were worn smooth by the loving hands that used them. The marks and scuffs on bowls, breadboxes, saltboxes, wooden rolling pins, heavy skillets and chipped coffee cups were the results of daily work performed out of care and concern and out of love for the strong growing family that ate its daily bread around the large inviting table at the center of the room.

Today, many kitchen accessories are mass-produced gadgets of coils and gears, switches and buttons—sleek machinery made of plastic or highly processed metals that buzzes and whirs. The most modern are digital and require only the slightest touch of the finger to set them in motion. When they are worn out, they look it and are thrown out and replaced with even newer models. They seldom invoke the fond memories and associations that the cruder accessories of yesteryear carried from generation to generation. And yet we cannot do without them. The kitchen is a collection of electrical gadgetry, and our lives have come to depend on the currents that run through the wires concealed in the walls of our homes. In many kitchens efficiency has replaced homeyness. The streamlined mixer that can be operated by a young child has replaced the strong, flour-dusted hands that stirred the mixing bowl.

One question regarding accessories, however, is perennial: where to store them? It's questionable whether older kitchens had more accessories than newer ones, or vice versa. But it's a fact that the newer devices are often more space-consuming than the older. The electric can opener cannot be thrown into the drawer with the knives and forks. The electric juicer cannot be stacked along with the plates like the little glass orange juice squeezer our grandmothers used. And the muscle power that produced those scrumptious meals appeared naturally wherever the cook was standing, unlike the electrical outlets that force certain activities to take place in areas where they supply the current needed for operating the gadgets and gizmos.

And how many gizmos there are—they seem to multiply overnight: juic-

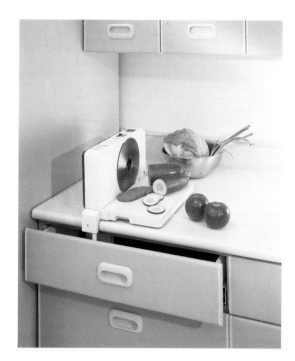

A golden rule for optimal kitchen layout is to provide adequate storage space and then to store items in or near the location where they will be used. This electric slicer, for instance, is a handy piece of equipment for the chef who prides himself or herself on the presentation of a meal as well as the taste. For a professional looking salad or meat tray, each piece must be uniformly sliced and, to many, the thinner the better. Kept in the drawer underneath when not in use, this portable slicer can be placed right on the counter nearby.

Many homeowners don't appreciate the cluttered look in a kitchen when small appliances are left out on open shelving. To them, the ideal kitchen is one that only looks cleaned up when everything is cleared away. And yet there are design limitations in some areas that will not allow for deep drawers or extra cabinets. How can those areas, such as under the overhead cabinets and against the backsplash, be utilized for storing small appliances? In this case, handy roller shades pull up and down to conceal equipment stored on small wire shelves beneath the regular cabinets. On the extreme left, see how this minicabinet looks when closed. To the right is an open section revealing bread, a toaster, eggbeater, and other items.

Here is a plain, old-fashioned looking kitchen with a variety of storage options. The traditional cabinetry has plain solid doors on most of the units except for the two sections in the corner by the window. These have glass doors because the items stored in them are attractive in their own right and add to the overall decor of the kitchen. For the same reason some of the dishware is displayed on clean wooden shelving on the other side of the window. Less attractive utensils can be kept behind the solid doors where they do not detract from the beauty of the room. Notice how attractively simple touches of blond wood highlight areas of the kitchen and offset the plain white tile and metal aura of the room.

Accessories can always be considered decorative touches when purchased with an eye for color, shape, and style. In this kitchen, dominated by two boldly contrasting colors, white and brown, items such as salad bowls, spoons, and a knife holder are as luxurious and integral to the overall decor as the fine Mexican pot or the richly woven carpet on the wall over the cabinets. The wood trim that accents the clean white decor is the key to the accessories and aesthetic details. Even a small detail such as the dark wooden handles on the knives was considered as a component in the general scheme.

ers, food processors, blenders, mixers, can openers, electric skillets, slow-cookers, microwaves, garbage disposals, compactors, toasters, ice makers, ice crushers, electric hot plates, bun warmers, popcorn poppers, coffee makers, etc. Several months before Christmas you will see advertisements on television for more outlandish contraptions that no one ever seems to actually have in their kitchen. Somewhere there must be a limit to the amount of electrical contrivances the average kitchen can accommodate. A hot dog will always be a hot dog, whether it is electrically

cooked from the inside out, fried in a pan, boiled in water, or held on a carved stick over an open fire.

*N*ot to be defeated by modernity, even the most up-to-date kitchens strive to retain a touch of the old days when meals seemed heartier and the kitchen more heart-warming. The decorative aspects of many accessories retain the old-world charm. Containers made of glass, wicker, or wire highlight many modern kitchens. Glass containers let you easily see what's in them, although some foods lose their color and freshness when exposed to

light. Wire baskets suspended from the ceiling allow vegetables to be well-ventilated and are easy reminders to family members to eat fresh nutritious apples, bananas, and oranges. Most fruit tastes richer at room temperature, anyway, and unless it will spoil before it is eaten, should not be stored in the refrigerator. Tin canisters have a unique charm about them as they can be painted or decorated to match your overall decor, changed easily when you tire of them, and the little dents and scuffs they receive speak well of a cook who still uses the flour, sugar, and baking ingredients in meals made

This kitchen has an irresistibly warm substantial look, snug and isolated from the busy world going by outside. This effect is created partially by the small window over the sink that looks out into another room, but also by the solid, durable quality of the major fixtures seen here. The commercial stove adds a marked note of worth and stability, as do other accessories such as the heavy chopping block used as a work surface in the middle of the room. This tabletop can accommodate the fierce pounding and chopping of meat or the delicate snip and cut of flower arranging. The old-fashioned ceiling fan and light fixture also recall styles that endure and are always welcome—whether in the past that we imagine must have been quieter than our own time or in the fast-paced future for which we are preparing.

The owner of the kitchen below makes violins, cellos, violas, and harpsichords in his studio at home. A musician himself, his surroundings reflect his love of musical instruments and motifs. Even the pots and pans displayed overhead resemble the notes on a musical scale or a culinary xylophone waiting to be played with a long wooden spoon. In the photo on the upper right, cookware is hung in a more traditional way. High above the work table, pots and pans are out of the way and yet within easy reach. A double-shelved pedestal in the center of this work island is ideal for spices. Located in Santa Fe, this bright and sunny kitchen reflects the open outdoor lifestyle that is so natural in the Southwest.

The dead space in corners where two sections of cabinetry are joined is an ideal space for storing small appliances. By installing lazy-Susan shelving, items never get lost in the recesses. It also makes sense to install a simple light in the storage space underneath large and deep counters, so the depths of the cupboards can be illuminated when you want to see into them.

from scratch. Perhaps the original "scratch" referred to the dents and scratches on tin canisters!

Cookware almost cries out to be hanged. Coming in remarkably diverse sizes and shapes, pots and pans never stack as easily as they appear to on the boxes manufacturers pack them in. At best they create precarious leaning towers of metal, get suctioned inside one another, and cause an enormous racket when you want to extract one from the bottom or middle. Face it, they are clunky, clanky, and cumbersome, so hang them from hooks on the wall or on overhead racks where they will lend a bright sparkle to your kitchen as they reflect light, but will be easy to reach when you need them. Some designers feel that cookware left out creates a cluttered look. True! But it is a clutter that honestly admits that the kitchen is a room that is in use almost continually. There's no real need to have the kitchen look artificially empty, as if no one ever cooks or eats in it. Of course, there is a point where accessories left on counters and tables become clutter not charm, sloppiness not efficiency. Salt and pepper condiments are fine left at the end of the kitchen table. An oregano jar left out looks messy.

*K*itchens, like bedrooms and bathrooms, create laundry, and in our generation of diminishing maid service, no one wants to do extra laundry. And so the usual linens—tablecloths, napkins, towels, dish rags, and place mats—that once lent a touch of warmth and assurance to kitchens have been replaced by paper products. Rather than colorful stacks of napkins or towels whose texture is interesting to see and touch, we now have stacks of paper in torn plastic wrappers. Real

linen hanging from hooks, or stacked on the counter, or spread over a table creates a comforting touch that paper can never match. Your personal napkin is like a friend waiting to greet you at each meal. Even the old tablecloth with the coffee stain that never came out becomes one of those little images that lends familiarity and personality to a family meal. The family linens produce memories, patterns and stains, colors and textures that stay with us as we grow up and begin families of our own. They contain memories that are not disposable, but are part of family legends and lore that are never thrown away.

Because the kitchen is in constant need of cleaning up, even after the simplest meals, detergents, cleansers, and other maintenance accessories are a must and need to be carefully stored. Left out they nudge our sensibilities even beyond the oregano not in its proper place in the spice rack. The obvious place for unaesthetic cleansers is under the sink where they are easily accessible when needed. Under the sink, however, is one of the great mysterious places of dark, damp Evil that toddlers love to explore! The lure of danger is uncontrollable even in two-year-olds, and where else in the kitchen would trolls hang out other than under the sink? Be sure that safety determines where you store poisonous cleansers as much as efficiency. Also remember that many cleansers are volatile if stored near flame, and some emit chemical odors that can spoil food and ruin the wonderful smells that give kitchens a great name.

*A*ntiques and kitchens fit together like a hand in a glove. Even in modern, space-age kitchens, one can usually find an occasional antique piece that somehow fits. Cooking and eating are two of the oldest human activities, so an antique egg beater or a third-generation napkin ring belongs even in a high-tech kitchen.

Food is the essence of human life and health. We are each the end product of a family food chain: our parents learned to prepare food from their parents, and so on, back to the faded origins of family histories. Because the need for food is so elementary, we are reminded and reassured by the old, well-used accessories that occasionally grace the cupboards and work areas of modern kitchens. Almost as if they have some magic that modern appliances and gadgets lack, these accessories magnetize our attention and entice us to pick them up, if for no other reason than to touch them, for a kitchen is above all an environment that is meant to be experienced, in every sense of that word.

And so we have come full circle. In spite of the fact that accessories come and go, appear and get thrown away, they all contribute to the life and atmosphere of the kitchen because it is a room of real feelings, a place where human drama is enacted and where life is sustained. Kitchen accessories are in their own way accessories for life and health. Whatever they have looked like in the past, whatever they will look like in the future, they sustain us as they contribute to the food we prepare, the meals we eat, the fun we have with each other in the kitchen.

Bold primary colors brighten up kitchens decorated in basic white and wood tones. The unpretentious wine and dish rack over the counter comes alive when filled with plastic plates, mugs, and a good supply of wines. Notice how other accessories such as canisters, cutting block, and paper-towel rack match the dominant blond wood.

This variation on the preceding kitchen does not allow accessories to break up the two-color pattern. Rather, the overall effect is more subdued and muted because the white dishware repeats the white and off-white tones of tile, counter, and major appliances. This kitchen epitomizes aesthetic efficiency.

Without the single shelf of earthy colors in white-capped spice jars standing at attention, this windowless end of a monochromatic kitchen would shine with only a dull gray tone. But with it, the area becomes friendlier and is an example of the Oriental technique of creating empty space that appears full in its very emptiness. And so this kitchen, devoid of numerous colors and utensils, seems adequately filled with spice jars and needs little else.

*The high-tech look can be a dominant style for a kitchen or merely
suggested by touches of industrial materials here and there. In this
kitchen the metal shelving and commercial cubicles replace
traditional cabinetry and open shelving. The modular bins are
designed to display their contents, and the owner has arranged the
various items in a nonchalant way. The vibrant red and yellow color
scheme keeps the room looking contemporary and upbeat.*

4

Decorative Touches

As in other rooms, decorative touches for the eighties might include the most traditional items or the most unusual. Today's home decorator need not feel constrained by the standards and styles of earlier generations. Anything goes—and with a little imagination almost anything can be made to fit. In this kitchen in Tennessee, the cook is no longer relegated to conventional surroundings three times a day. A bright neon sculpture emblazoned on a brick wall marries the pulsating beat of urban life with the warm earth colors of brick. As with so many contemporary lifestyles, the effect is a winning blend of the natural and the manmade.

The Los Angeles film producer who cooks in this kitchen has allowed his love of black-and-white movies to influence his interior design choices. The black ceramic tile work surfaces and the dark stove stand out boldly against the dusty white color of the walls. Resembling a miniature screen for a screening room, the black-and-white photo on the wall is the only necessary decoration. It is the focal point of the entire end of the room, pulling the eye to a center as the principle of perspective might work in a Whistler painting.

The kitchen poses unique challenges for interior decoration because much of the available wall space is hidden by large appliances. There is also the problem of floor space and how to keep the floor clear for traffic passing through, as well as for the constant walking from stove to sink to fridge while preparing meals. What look like table tops waiting for a piece of sculpture, a floral bouquet, or some other objet d'art are really work spaces that can't be cluttered up with beauty. Furthermore, the kitchen is subject to steam, greasy fumes, and warm temperatures—climatic conditions that discourage people from filling the room with expensive or delicate pieces of artwork.

And yet, because the kitchen needs so many accessories and contains so many distinct areas, the challenge of applying decorative touches is not as frustrating as it may appear. In fact, decorating a kitchen is fun because there is so much that can be done with the most utilitarian objects and spaces. What would look inappropriate in a living room or entrance foyer becomes charming and clever when aesthetically adapted to the kitchen.

A key guideline for kitchen decoration is to keep in mind that it is a room which must lift one's spirits. So much time is spent in it doing repetitive, unexciting tasks that the cook or dishwasher relies on the surroundings to provide motivation and inspiration on those days and nights when one's heart is just not in the job that must be done. Furthermore, the overall ambiance must not grow tiresome for the family who will spend many hours of many days in the kitchen. Some family members eat all three meals there and expect a setting that accommodates the range of hours and moods, from sleepy breakfasts in winter, to quick

Artwork has become a more popular element of kitchen decor in recent years as kitchens have become more spacious and better ventilated. In the kitchen below, a gallery of favorite prints adorns the dining area and other available wall spaces, even at the working end of the room. In the kitchen on the right, one large piece of nonrepresentational artwork in startling primary colors graces the ceiling. The somber aura of this kitchen of dark industrial tones and materials is alleviated as the eye and spirit are drawn upward. The bright colors overhead illuminate simple objects like red potholders and yellow bananas lower down.

lunches in summer, to elegant dinners for celebrating a birthday or anniversary. The decor must suit even late-night snacks. Whether you decorate your kitchen sensibly or extravagantly, the design of the room becomes part of the mealtime experience, so don't count on hunger to dull the aesthetic senses. The taste that satisfies the eye can be as important as that which pleases the palate.

The kitchen requires many accessories, so always bear in mind their aesthetic impact when you select them. They need not be expensive, but they should coordinate well with basic color, patterns, and themes. A well-stocked kitchen boutique contains an impressive array of merchandise (salt and pepper shakers, honey pots, cookie jars, spice racks, towels, knife holders, and so forth) that will satisfy the most utilitarian needs and the most demanding sense of design. In addition to the practical reasons for having these items in the kitchen, aesthetic considerations should never be overlooked. Each accessory and decorative object will be part of the overall mosaic that makes up the design of your kitchen. For example, cookery hanging on the wall or overhead racks could sport the copper bottoms that echo other copper objects in the room, such as planters, cookie cutters, or mugs. Their warm glowing surfaces will catch the light, and add amber color and sparkle.

*E*very room nowadays seems to sprout plants. Greenery has invaded the home, bringing the freshness and naturalness of the out-of-doors inside, where we need it. What better room to suggest the irrepressible vitality of nature than a kitchen alive with healthy growing plants and flowers? Common objects that would look drab and out of place in other rooms take on a kind of magic in the kitchen—old teapots and coffee mugs for planters, grandma's old canisters for ferns, even a sprig taking root in a few inches of water in a simple, clear glass jar seems to belong on the shelf near a kitchen window. This is the room for growth and nourishment. Dried herbs and flowers complement the essence of kitchen activities, suggesting the abundance of the harvest months when nature's bounty bestows the fruits of a successful growing season. And don't overlook fresh fruit for decorative touches; it changes with the seasons of the year, and reminds your hungry family that there are better between-meal snacks than junk food bought from vending machines.

Many food products make attractive displays for the various nooks in a well-used kitchen. For instance, pasta in glass jars of various sizes lends a ribbed and ruffled texture to a plain wall. The earthy colors of spices and herbs afford a pleasant contrast to a wall painted either white or another bright color. And vegetables that do not need refrigeration, such as potatoes, turnips, onions, and carrots create a down-home table setting when artfully arranged in a wooden bowl. Hung from the ceiling in wire baskets, they approximate the earthy patience of a root cellar or a walk-in pantry.

Since so many areas in the kitchen are sleek and smooth, it makes good decorating sense to incorporate other textures wherever possible. The cold smooth tiles, while they can be colorful in themselves, need some contrast, for example, wicker or wood. The natural material of wicker makes a comfortable background for food, and creates a clean, ventilated motif when used in baskets for fruit, food trays, or

The delightfully haphazard way Memphis-style furniture combines offbeat colors and slightly skewed shapes is exemplified by this round glass-top table stand. Other happy-go-lucky touches are clearly evident in the blue gauzy fruit bowl, the mosaic tile border that trims the backsplash, the tea kettles and mugs atop the cabinets, and other items of interest. The plain funnel-shaped light fixture hangs knotted on its chord, and the entire room takes on a special informality and friendliness not found in more staid and sober kitchens. With a slightly nostalgic look, this kitchen speaks openly about the childhood joys of growing up in the 1950s.

A study in beige and copper, this kitchen is a successful collaboration of two artists, one who created the etched-glass cabinet doors, the other who transformed this small space into a clean, well-lighted cooking area. The single window dispenses bright sunlight, muted by a plain white sheer curtain for a soft glowing effect that harmonizes with the beautiful autumn shine of copper on the pots and pans and the quiet light from an ornate lamp.

Stenciling is an ancient art dating back over one thousand years to China, where some of the earliest examples are of Buddhist religious themes. In the Western world, the art has gone through many secular transformations over the centuries and today is often associated with primitive folk crafts. Here is a magnificent example of how the old decorative techniques can stage their comeback with boldness and splendor. The owners of this eighteenth-century home in Connecticut commissioned a noted Scottish church decorator to recreate one of their favorite Oriental rugs in a trompe l'oeil by cutting stencils for the medallions of the original rug.

Necessity is often the mother of ingenious accomplishment in home design. This New York kitchen opens onto an unattractive alleyway, but the designer turned that liability into one of the most appealing features of this room. A frosted-glass window tinted blue provides a bright restful backdrop for a modest green plant. The air conditioner was installed overhead to allow for a more aesthetic view at eye level and to avoid becoming an annoyance to those seated at the table with their backs exposed to the blast of air. Determined to transform a potentially viewless and ''dead'' area of the room into an attractive nook for dining, the owner was stunningly successful with a simple, inexpensive arrangement.

Clean, softly illuminated, and strikingly simple in its decor, this kitchen exudes a healthy sense of care and concern for what is both hygienic and attractive. The rather cozy area avoids any feeling of cramped oppressiveness by the breakthroughs of light in the recessed sections of the ceiling. Beams are directed over the most frequently used work areas by cutouts in the framework ceiling structure. The Connecticut designers who live here have achieved a pleasing, utilitarian ambiance that is nevertheless aesthetically seductive. A modicum of color and light tones keep the room interesting and comfortable. Here is a room that is formal enough for entertaining guests and yet casually inviting for family and young people, a room that can bounce back from almost any occasion.

place mats; it also looks great when coordinated with wicker-backed chairs. Rugs can define various areas of the kitchen by altering the texture of the floor. Not only will they ease the pressure on the feet in areas where you stand a lot, but they add color and pattern to complement or contrast with other themes. Spatter-pattern rugs are best for not showing spills and crumbs, but if your basic floor design is splatter-pattern, then solid-colored rugs should be used. Even the mat inside the back door for wiping feet can become part of an overall mood of friendliness that welcomes your guest or neighbor into the warmth and coziness of your kitchen.

Kitchen windows were made to be as open and airy as possible, never obscured by heavy curtains. Café curtains were designed purposely to allow as much sunlight as possible to enter, yet still afford some privacy. In addition to café curtains, loosely woven full-length curtains, decorative shades such as Roman or Austrian styled, or narrow, tinted high-tech blinds can adorn kitchen windows for aesthetic purposes, as well as for ease in adjusting the amount of light or privacy needed for various types of meals and kitchen-table activities.

Where you have room on a bare wall for a wall hanging, consider the use of posters and graphics. While they may appear utilitarian in other rooms of the house, they are always in style in most kitchens. Pictures of famous restaurants and cafés, stylized illustrations of fruit, vegetables, pastries, and food-related themes, even still-life drawings of kitchen objects such as pots and pans, or tea kettles and cups, fit right in without overdoing the basic idea of the kitchen. More than other rooms, the kitchen seems to want to be what

An old deteriorating factory building that stands in the East End of London has become a whimsical and somewhat funky place of residence under the new owner's architectural daring. The open-truss wooded roof and walls were left intact to retain the authentic character of the building. Offbeat odds-and-ends and bargains discovered at local flea markets enhance the easy-going quality that gives the kitchen its identity. It is a hybrid hollow for the serious hobo and the eccentric antique collector. Hanging pots, pans, and fish kettles from the ceiling alleviates storage problems and adds to the wacky charm.

it is—a kitchen, delighting in its own reflection and purposes. Creative homemakers can find unique and intriguing patterns and pictures for kitchen art. Many product labels, especially the ones that have acquired a legendary aura in Americana, such as Campbell's soup, Jello, Quaker Oats, Morton salt, and Maxwell House coffee, can add a little whimsy and nostalgia to even the most modern kitchen when mounted and framed. A gallery of popular brand-name foods over a cabinet or around a window in a breakfast nook can add fresh primary color and cartoon sensibility. But don't let your imagination remain confined in the traditional "kitcheny" themes and motifs. Bold, daring effects can be achieved by prints and sculpture that are not associated with the kitchen, such as erotic or historical artwork, or a photo gallery of your friends and relatives.

Another innovative do-it-yourself design strategy is to cut the basic pattern elements out of extra wallpaper and affix them to cabinets or the backs of chairs. This lifts the general motif off the wall and extends it to the interior spaces of the room. In lieu of wallpaper, any stencil that makes the statement you want to see repeated throughout certain areas of your kitchen will do the trick and pull the room together.

*A*ntique hunting offers unlimited design ideas for the kitchen. Whether you snoop through flea markets and antique shops for the "real McCoy" or merely decorate and furnish your kitchen with "antique-style" accessories, the shapes, colors, and patterns of yesteryear never seem out of place. A shelf or mantel of pewter plates, mugs, and candlesticks recaptures the colonial days when craftsmanship was nearly perfect and the crafts people took as much pride in their work as the thoughtful cook should take in preparing meals. Old pottery can always be used practically in a kitchen, and it will also serve as an object of art or conversation.

Larger pieces of antique furniture are one way to combine storage space with attractive furnishings. China cabinets can hold dishware, linens, extra sets of utensils; and an old-fashioned

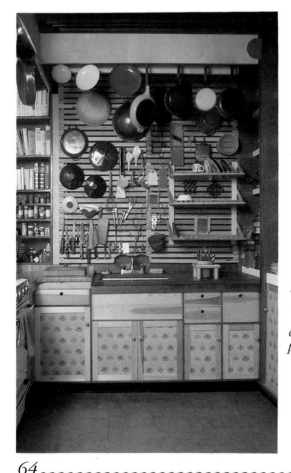

The accessories on this kitchen wall climb right up from the counter to the ceiling. The wooden rack provides a steady pattern to offset the distracted array of colors and shapes. Here is a kitchen that because of the consciously achieved, cluttered effect never looks truly cluttered or messy. It's a kitchen ideally decorated for the no-nonsense cook who wants equipment within reach and no fussy art objects or precious knickknacks to move out of the way. Again we see a kitchen whose predominant wood design is accented by splashes of bold bright colors, and one that is totally decorated with practical kitchen items.

Unlike the kitchen on the left, whose storage technique encompasses contemporary urban products, this kitchen spot envelops the aura of another time and place. In it are the commercial products of yesteryear, tastefully preserved and arranged on antique shelving. Here is a mood of quiet sensitivity to the quality of the past—to Mason jars, Dutch ovens, canned goods. This setting speaks of days spent preparing and preserving foods for large growing families in a kitchen that respects the past and the older values not totally lost in modern life.

pie-cooling cabinet can function as a china cabinet! Every kitchen that serves a large growing family needs coat racks near the door, boot boxes for rainy or snowy days, and the indispensable umbrella rack. A twig chair or foot stool near the back door can be used for putting on boots or simply to set a bag of groceries on while you latch the door or let the dog out.

For light and ventilation, the old ceiling fan or fan-and-light combination is perfect for keeping the air moving through the room on days of heavy baking or on days when *you* are baking because of the summer heat. Many kitchen designers have solved the question of what material to use on those walls (and ceilings too) that collect grease and steam by using pressed tin behind stoves and around sinks where soapy water can splash and leave unsightly streaks if not frequently wiped clean.

*W*hatever you decide for your interior decor, remember that the kitchen is a busy room. There are only a few moments each day (usually when no one is in them anyway) when kitchens are not being used for some purpose or another. Just like the people who traipse through the kitchen, the equipment you use and the objects that adorn the walls and counters always seem to be on the move. Nothing stands still. Like hunger, which returns with clocklike regularity several times a day, the decorative touches of the kitchen should be magnets that draw the eye as well as the mind to the wholesome, satisfying activities for which we build our kitchens in the first place. In a room used by every member of the family, the color and design and the motifs and statements, whether elegant or humorous, expensive or down-home, formal or come-as-you-are, should have a universal appeal that can be appreciated by all. For, in the final analysis, it is the camaraderie and relaxation of mealtime that creates the quintessential dining experience. The dried herbs on the wall, the ceiling fan overhead, the twig rocker in the corner, the clowns and cut-outs on the refrigerator door are merely the setting for the comfort and pleasure of eating well and enjoying one another's company.

What better decorations for the kitchen than natural food products, arranged and displayed in a setting that does not pretend to be anything but a place where food is prepared, cooked, and served? This kitchen's most appealing touches are the pasta in tall slender jars; the glass canisters filled with baking ingredients such as salt, pepper, flour, and corn meal; a long row of squat little jars containing herbs, spices, and nuts; and two wire baskets filled to the rim with potatoes, onions, and juicy red apples. Glass, clay pottery, and glazed earthenware items rest behind the cabinet's glass doors. In this kitchen both decor and accessories seem all of one theme, expressing this cook's love of the earth and its nutritious bounty.

Like its partner on the left, this kitchen sprouts an array of foliage—but with a difference. The dense jungle-effect created by large, leafy plants is allowed to grow in an untamed manner, conveying a sense that green things have a right to be here. Letting nature have her way solves the problem of how to decorate a corner of a kitchen or to block an unappealing view through a large window. The natural profusion of plants also creates privacy without curtains or blinds. In this kitchen a skylight and floor-length windows provide the necessary light for maximal growth.

For the avid gardener, a conservatory off the kitchen area makes a lot of sense. Close to water and wash-up materials, a long narrow alcove such as this one lets you fuss with plants while keeping an eye on preparing the meals. Spacious skylights and large windows provide ample sunlight, and the proximity to a patio makes it easy to move plants outside for seasonal change of habitat. There's no need to mention the lush green view from the sink and counter that lessens the drudgery of cleaning up after meals. This garden center is made of easy-to-clean materials that can withstand the unavoidable spills and splashes when tending to household plants.

When remodeling a large old kitchen, turn one corner of it into a place for a favorite hobby or craft. This area has become a workroom for the gardener-herbalist who loves to grow exotic plants, dry flowers, and create handcrafted items of beauty from dessicated stalks, leaves, and brambles. Other plants and herbs are ground with a pestle and mortar and put up for cooking needs in the seasons ahead. This crafts room is well-stocked with all the equipment and paraphernalia needed, including places to suspend plants and bulbs during the drying process. The red highlights of the stools, lamp, faucet, and the patterned tile of the sink and work table, add a touch of contemporary verve to the natural, old-fashioned beauty of the room.

Hand-painted ceramic tiles decorated with foods and flowers liven up this rustic kitchen, bringing the charm of rural France to this sideboard. The provocative French language lends romance and glamor to the rather mundane objects depicted here. But as with the finest gourmet meal, the very ordinary can become a rare dish when prepared with the infinite care of a French chef. The overall effect is that this sideboard and sunken brazier become a special place, with extra plates stacked underneath, guarded by two enormous clay pots and a rather supercilious ceramic cat who seems to insist on being the chat of the chateau.

The solid blond wood cabinetry in this kitchen is trimmed with black metal and tile to create an effect of timeless elegance. The black metal handles and side borders lend an almost Japanese flavor to the bleached oak cabinets. The black tile counters and backsplash provide a smart area for food preparation and cleanup. The owners have enhanced the black-on-blond color scheme by carefully selecting dishware, the light fixture, and other kitchen items to share the rich black tones and highlight areas such as corner shelves and place settings at the table. Dark ceiling and floor materials encapsulate the entire room so the furnishings glow with a steady vibrance.

Many kitchen designs today seek to blend the old and new, but sometimes it's hard to locate antique or weathered materials that have stood the test of time and are still serviceable. Fortunately, we can treat new materials with modern aging processes so they acquire that antique charm. The perforated, hammered sheet tin that make these lower cabinets so attractive is not old but actually brand new. Rubbed down with muriatic acid, these panels have "aged" in look if not in substance, and now they recapture the distant look of cabinetry from an earlier era.

5
Dining Areas

Somewhere in or near the kitchen is the place where judgment is passed on the cook's efforts—the eating area. Whether it is a complete dining room, a breakfast alcove, a service counter, or the traditional kitchen table at one end of the room, a comfortable, friendly place is a must for a successful kitchen. Today's homes usually have more than one dining place, often a formal dining room for important occasions located in a room away from the kitchen proper in addition to a more informal setting usually in or extending from the kitchen for quick family meals and impromptu snacks. The elegant eating area shown here demonstrates how a small space utilizing a conventional booth construction can be a luxurious place to sit and enjoy a meal or late afternoon cocktail. The burnished metal and smoked-glass table exudes a quiet dignity matched by the gray overstuffed seats that ring it.

The hours spent "slaving away in a hot kitchen"—reduced considerably in recent years by microwave ovens, instant meals, and frozen dinners—are worthwhile if the end product is a delicious meal that will be enjoyed by your loved ones. The *raison d'être* for the expensive appliances and accessories that comprise modern kitchens is to produce nourishing dinners for yourself, your family, and your friends. At least as much time, attention, and care should be devoted to developing a relaxing and comfortable dining area as is used in planning an efficient work space for cooking the meals and cleaning up afterwards. A clean, well-lighted place is the ideal eating environment for everyone, and lucky are those people who have kitchens with ample windows along a wall, in a bay window area, or a comfortable corner where they can create the perfect setting for enjoying mealtimes together.

The dining area should be at least psychologically distinct from the rest of the kitchen if it cannot always be physically separate. Face it, some kitchens are too small or the room design does not lend itself well to creating a separate eating nook. But whether you add on a distinct dining room or family room for meals, or merely convert a cozy corner into a breakfast alcove, every household needs a haven of relaxation and rest in the kitchen, close to snack food, cold drinks, and cups of coffee for "nourishment" breaks in the course of a busy day. Working around the home requires time-outs to pause and reflect and get one's wits together before going back to the tasks that must be done. A cup of herbal tea before putting the laundry in the dryer, a bottle of beer while mowing the lawn, an after-school snack of granola bars and juice to tide the kids over until dinner, or a glass of milk before bed are just as important in a busy day as are the major chores and responsibilities.

Sometimes the decision as to how extensive the eating area will be is made on the cook's preference: should the kitchen be an open kitchen or a closed one? Open kitchens are so designed that they extend hearty and obvious invitations to family and friends to drop in and chat with the cook. Chairs are always ready, high stools stand near the work space, and the major appliances are arranged with plenty of room between for someone to come in and visit, leaning against the counters, out of the cook's way. Some cooks—even busy ones—love company.

Others prefer isolation, using the time to be alone to concentrate on new recipes. They anticipate the hours it takes to prepare a meal as a time to be by themselves. For them, the kitchen should incorporate a closed design with the eating area removed or screened off from the work areas. Both types of kitchens can accommodate eating areas, but in the case of a closed kitchen more concern must be taken to provide the cook with the necessary visual or audial privacy.

The most open type of kitchen was the traditional farmhouse kitchen with a large square table smack in the center. The solid commodious table served as a work counter during food preparation and as a dining table during meals. Several chairs were always clustered around it. Farmwives enjoyed children or workers dropping in when passing by the house, or neighbors who stopped by to exchange chit chat and recipes. Today, a large table placed in the center of the kitchen is not in style, even though the concept

This kitchen looks like an elegantly designed space module ready for liftoff. And yet it is a room very much of this world, whose regalness excludes any suggestion of fast-food or frozen meals. The outer hemisphere is a gleaming marble counter, with a base made of oriental rattan that matches the panels on the cabinet doors and the casing for the range hood. The centrifugal design is reproduced in the circular cooking island in the middle and in the tubular range hood itself.

All eating counters do not have to be small areas that can seat only two or three people comfortably. Here is an extended tabletop reaching out of the service counter that can easily seat six or more. A long table in its own right, the solid white laminated material is the same as the cabinet and shelf structure in the work area. A white-ribbed light fixture hangs over the table and matches the white wire shelf design. Because of the plain white decor in the cabinet and table modules, almost any style chair would fit right in. Here, unfinished wooden upright chairs seem ready-made for the place. And yet more extravagantly designed and patterned chairs would work too.

The personality of this kitchen is partially attributable to the deep grove of trees just outside, but the designer's imagination was at sea rather than in the forest. Here is an eating nook patterned after a nautical style. Even the sleek phone and control panels on the right look as if they were developed for an environment where every square inch of space must be utilized in the most unobtrusive manner. The laminated wood seats extend up and over the table, with a break for overhead lights. The result is a cozy, secluded nook for time-out from regular daily activities, even if they do not include hoisting a mainsail or "falling off the wind."

This eating counter has so much character it could play several roles. As a dining table for two, it is a handsomely carved three-sided arrangement that allows you to sit facing your partner while eating rather than the wall. When you are alone, this alcove surrounds you with your favorite books, a small television, and a phone on which to chat with a friend while you eat. In fact, when the dishes are cleared away, this elegant little area is comfortable enough to be used for writing letters, jotting down plans for the next day, or casual reading. The recessed light in the corner provides ample soft lighting for eating as well as for other activities. It's a small but luxurious setting that can easily seduce you into spending long pleasant hours there.

has been retained in the island structures that may be used for working, cooking, and eating. A combination work-and-dining complex in the middle of the room is convenient for the cook and provides the immediate space needed for quick snacks or speedy lunches. High stools or chairs can be used for eating, then can be removed or slid under the counter when it is being used for slicing vegetables or cutting up meats. In some kitchens the island work area is in fact the divider that separates the dining area from the rest of the kitchen. It then becomes a handy service counter and a place to stack dirty dishes after a

meal on their way to the sink or dishwasher.

In keeping with today's kitchen designs, informal eating spaces are located at one end of the kitchen and are separate from the dining room where more formal entertaining takes place. These family dining areas may be along a wall, tucked into a corner, or situated in a bay window. Even small kitchenettes need some eating area; it could be a fold down table, a small bar, or any available counter space. Preferably, counters should face out a window or into the next room so that you won't face the wall at each meal. A problem with most counters is that

two people sharing breakfast or lunch together must both face the same way. If space permits, use a half-moon table so that the two of you might turn a little toward each other.

A favorite kitchen spot for family meals is the booth built into a bay window or a dormer nook. Built-in bench seats save space and can be made with removable and washable seat pads. The problem of crawling in and out of booths can be eliminated by putting the table on castors and attaching it to the wall with springs, thus allowing a twelve-inch swing space for entering and leaving. If the dining space is extremely confined, a

The convenience of having more than one eating place near the kitchen is seen in this arrangement. For fast meals alone or with one other companion, the service counter will suffice. For full family meals or when entertaining another couple, the round table and rattan chairs by the window make a nice, out-of-the-way dining space. Both places reflect the austere simplicity of the decor characterized by clean open spaces. The entire area has a beauty that does not need more than a single blossom and two napkins to lend grace and color. The window in the dining area wraps up into the ceiling, bringing the outdoors in.

In a similar vein, this dining area needs very little beyond the basic furniture. Of course, here, the magnificence of nature becomes a breathtaking backdrop for meals. The all-white setting lets the seasonal colors outdoors and the lofty sweep of sky dominate. No need to fear inclement weather here; you can experience the refreshing pleasure and beauty of dining outdoors even on rainy or snowy days.

glass-top table won't dominate the area, nor will it make the area look cramped, as would a solid table that visually blocks the walls and floor. Being able to see through the table makes it almost disappear, and the overall effect is roomy and airy. For more formal dining, a floor-length tablecloth thrown over a table-top will add an elegant touch. Also, more people can fit at a round table in a small area than can huddle around a square table. If the table has a pedestal base rather than four legs, it will be more comfortable when you need to squeeze an extra friend in for dinner. No one has to suffer the discomfort of straddling a table leg.

A well-lighted eating area is a must for growing families, not only so the children can see what they are eating and develop good eating habits, but also to accommodate the many non-mealtime activities that take place at the table: homework, coloring books, cut-outs, board games, and your own poker or canasta clubs. Nevertheless, every couple, even those with young children, needs a romantic dinner alone once in a while; the intensity of the light should be adjustable in order to turn the eating place into something special for those fantasy occasions requiring a certain amount of shadow and the flicker of candlelight. A Tiffany-style lamp with a dimmer switch and adjustable height can satisfy all a family's lighting needs.

In some kitchens it is not possible to build a physically distinct area for meals, but much can be done with imaginative decorating schemes. Your dining space can always be aesthetically distinct from the kitchen's work areas even if it is physically the same room. It can be designed to create a distinct space. For example, a brick

Not every dining area can accommodate large substantial furnishings. In many cases when the eating area is actually part of a larger living or playroom, you may want the table and chairs to be as inconspicuous as possible. Or you may want wall hangings or other decorative objects to be the center of attention. If so, select a glass table that will practically disappear against the rest of the decor. In this kitchen the octagonal glass table with a tubular base of glass helps the area to retain a satisfyingly empty look. The eye is drawn to the artwork on the wall or the unified feel of the room as a whole without undue distraction from the table. Of course when set with a mouthwatering meal, the table itself recedes from attention even more.

This kitchen is part of a home built in an abandoned stable in a London mews. Because the building is almost windowless on three sides, a towering arched doorway reaching to the upper floors was constructed to admit as much daylight as possible. The kitchen, on an upper floor, includes a meal counter not designed for those who suffer from vertigo! The spiral staircase, banister, and three hanging light fixtures sport the high-tech look in bold primary colors. The circular steps are covered in black rubber tread and harmonize well with the small round windows, the archway, and black eating counter.

façade or wood panelling will suggest an entirely different room if it is opposed to the tile or wallpaper that dominates the rest of the kitchen. A change in the wallpaper around the table may be all you need. Many kitchens denote the dining area by varying the floor pattern of the tile or by carpeting the floor in the eating nook while using vinyl for easy maintenance on the remaining sections of the floor. If you have a large spacious kitchen, the dining area can extend logically and aesthetically from the major motif.

When renovating an old house, don't pass up the chance to convert large walk-in pantries or linen closets into breakfast rooms. Some older homes even have a small maid's room off the kitchen that can be made into a family dining room. In newer homes, an alternative strategy is to extend the kitchen area out onto the back porch or patio. Knock out a wall, expand a doorway, or build a half-wall to function as a room divider and serving counter and you will have a separate and distinct dining space.

However you achieve it, the guiding principle for most people is to have the eating place as close to the kitchen as possible; this allows for easier serving of hot food, and fast trips to the stove for seconds or to the fridge for dessert. But the flip side of this guideline is to have the eating area as far removed, at least visually, from the clutter of the sink, dirty dishes, pots and pans, and leftovers. Efficiency is a primary concern, but so is ambiance, because the sharing of food with another is meant to be a relaxing, refreshing ritual during the day. Where you eat can be as important as what you eat.

Take care that the place you provide for family meals has the qualities that will make everyone eager to join one another at dinner time. It should take place in a permanent spot in the home that lures us to it because it "feels" right, just as the food cooking on the stove lures us towards it with an irresistible aroma.

Teak wood and stony creek granite unify this dining place and its companion kitchen. The concave panels of the furnishings contrast with the sharp angular planes of the room itself. The cabinetry and table, with its half-moon headboard, soften the sharp corners of the walls, windows, and skylight. The mosaic floor of the kitchen proper extends only to the table, announcing subtly that the eating area is as much out of the kitchen as it is a part of it. Fronting the table against the wall, rather than using a freestanding table here, matches the design concept of the curved marble backsplash in the kitchen.

Here is another example of how marble can make even an island structure as elegant as a formal dining room table. This curved counter, dropped several inches below the work surface, is large enough to seat four people comfortably. The cane-bottomed chairs are curved in design so they cluster right up around the eating surface, visually and physically cozy for intimate meals. In fact the great success of this Bermuda kitchen stems from the eating facility that is so thoroughly isolated from the more austere work places in the room, creating a truly elegant and intimate area.

6

Unusual Arrangements

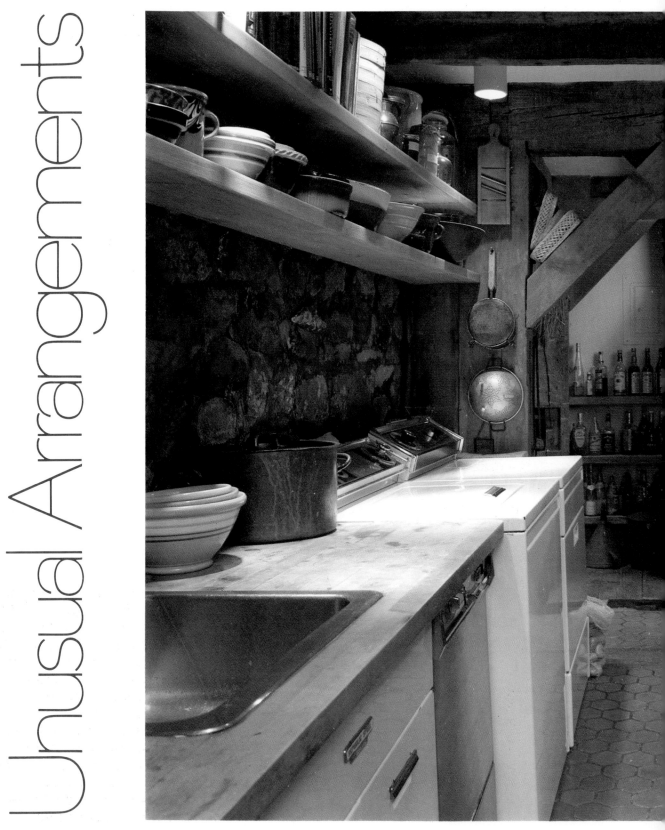

One of the joys of living in a converted millhouse is that just about anything goes—and pretty well at that! Here is the all-purpose scullery, laundry, pantry, and well-stocked bar, clustered around the now-immobile water wheel that once turned in the river's current. Certainly an unusual arrangement for a kitchen, it provides one of the more interesting alternatives to a standard set-up. Although the trend for many people of the eighties is toward simplicity, these allpurpose rooms that don't follow any standard of fashion or design offer a refreshing chance at individuality. When the stodgy rules of decorum are water under the bridge, old grocery bags can be wedged into a basket and a humble blue work apron will look fine hanging on a nail in the doorway.

We live in an age when what was formerly considered unusual is becoming more ordinary from day to day. In fact, it takes a strong leap of the imagination to devise something truly startling and innovative. Because our century has been marked by ingenuity on so many levels, it becomes exceedingly difficult to tap into your own "genius" for an idea that has not already been tried, tested, and now treated as nothing very remarkable. Kitchens in one form or another have been around for a long time. Their central role in family life and home architecture has been exploited by the well-known designers competing for novel ideas, as well as by the average homeowner, who makes improvements and additions every few years as the family grows and changes. Still, there is unexplored territory ahead for those who think beyond the ordinary kitchen.

Some of the best and most unusual arrangements are born of necessity. Trying to make the pressing demands of a kitchen fit an unkitchen-like space can bring out the heroic architect in each of us. Ovens, refrigerators, sinks, plumbing, gas lines, cabinets, and a place to sit down and eat—all in one room? It has been done. And those who have succeeded at it admit that it's not like creating a sitting room or another bedroom or even installing a commode in a small closet. Kitchens are massive projects that require massive doses of imaginative thinking, especially when adapting certain kitchen elements to other rooms and areas in the home. A wet bar in the family room, an extra refrigerator and snack area off the porch (so the children can get their own soft drinks and popsicles on hot summer days), or the extra grill or barbeque area near the patio or screened-in porch—each of these take

Often loft dwellers throw great parties! And if they don't, it certainly isn't because they don't have the room for a great bash! This New York loft is set up for a rather elegant celebration, and the kitchen itself is lost in the loveliness. Hovering on the far left are the actual kitchen facilities, and in the center back is the buffet counter ready with wine, champagne, and a chafing dish. Overhead track lights, which blend superbly with the pipes and beams of the ceiling and are usually angled to illuminate the kitchen area, are now aimed at the guest tables and the lavish buffet. This photographer's home is set up "pretty as a picture"—a lesson for those who entertain at home whether or not anyone comes with a camera.

When the owners of this London home considered the various ways to divide the space, an alternative occurred to them that wouldn't strike most of us—steel and slats! And so this architect couple constructed the various rooms of their home with interior steel frames and Venetian blinds. They carried through this theme with modern metal-framed chairs, a steel-slatted lamp, and open shelving above the countertops and desk. The high-tech result is true to the open plan that allows for easy flow of traffic, smooth circulation of air and light, and an expansive friendly atmosphere. Because the effects are virtually limitless, each room can be adjusted for whatever mood or activity is desired and interior designing is an ongoing process.

planning, know-how, and a certain daring.

The opposite of scattering kitchen facilities to other parts of the house is to bring the rest of the house into the kitchen. And why not? If the kitchen is truly the ersatz hearth for twentieth-century families, many home activities could take place surrounded by its warmth and comfort. It no longer has to be a room reserved for standing over stoves, wolfing down meals, and doing the dishes. For example, the television has invaded the kitchen as it has almost every other room in the house, including the bedroom and bathroom. Judging from the percentage of commercials that are about food, drink, nutrition, cleansers, shiny floors, and spotless glasses, a visitor from a strange planet might draw the conclusion that television was invented for the kitchen!

Also it is fairly common today to find a desk, a small shelf of books, and assorted office supplies in a secluded alcove of the kitchen. Turning a collection of cookbooks into a slightly broader range of reading materials was a natural development. Then, other things kept slipping in—a desk for composing shopping lists, taking phone messages (yes, a kitchen without a phone is an anomaly!), some stationery, and perhaps a typewriter for catching up on correspondence while waiting for the pasta to cook. And because it's difficult to look at all the kitchen appliances and not be reminded of the monthly utility bills, why not pay them in the kitchen?

*A*s technology creeps into more and more of our daily spaces, the television will evolve into a larger entertainment center, pehaps with stereo equipment, strategically angled speakers, and the necessary shelving space to house cassettes, video tapes, and record albums. The pen and stationery, if not already booted out by an electric typewriter, are being replaced in some kitchens by a word processor. In fact, the kitchen may well become the home media center. If you are paying the bills there, and your home computer is linked to your bank, why not have all the electronic maid-butler-secretary services located in the kitchen where historically they have been placed? Actually, finding room for the various electronic equipment and paraphernalia is another challenge for the interior designer. Some homes are already beginning to place all the large technological appliances in one room, and those who don't have the luxury of a media room are placing the growing number of electronic components in whatever room is available—in some cases, the kitchen.

Bringing unusual items into or near the kitchen is the outgrowth of three trends that have characterized urban living in the last generation: the efficiency apartment, the family room, and the loft. All three have encouraged and initiated modern families into relearning what our ancestors knew and presumably appreciated centuries ago—namely, that family activities are more relaxed and spontaneous when they can arise naturally in an informal setting around the space associated with nourishment, companionship, and love. In olden days it was the hearth; now it is the kitchen. As more of us live in small efficiency apartments (although we eventually outgrow them and long for more spacious accommodations), we learn that there is really something warm and cozy about being able to satisfy so many human needs in one compact area.

Some modern homes still have secret chambers and passageways. Beneath this hidden trap door is a well-stocked wine cellar. The pine flooring is ideal for such mysteries, for it is virtually impossible to spot the cracks in the floorboards, and a throw rug spread over the door would conceal the secret completely. Utilizing space beneath the floor makes sense, especially since wine should remain at a uniformly cool temperature. But the concept could easily be extended to fruit cellars or underground larders for canned goods. There's no need to waste valuable space upstairs if an entire basement lies empty. The trap door and ladder design is easy to use, and you literally have food—or drink—right at your feet.

Underground wine cellars and second floor kitchens! The traditional and the nontraditional! This kitchen, dining area, and sitting room are built on the second floor, away from the other rooms of the house. The curved wall of glass brick gently folds the kitchen and eating space into the sitting room for conversation after dinner or for relaxation while good things are cooking. A track of theatrical light fixtures over the stairwell lets the owners adjust the lighting effect for any mood or purpose—shining on the stairway for safety or on the dining table for atmosphere or on the back wall for dramatic effects. A ficus tree grows up from the stairwell, its leafy top branches adding to the decor of the second floor.

The stunning kitchen on p. 16 is seen here from farther away and at a different angle. This view includes the wet bar that is a twin companion in style and design to the main kitchen area. The audio command system overhead allows the owner to select whatever music he or she desires. Guests will be entertained by a small television screen while the chef prepares the evening meal. Cooking in this home, which is buttressed by the latest technology, should not be overly taxing, since the entire kitchen is computerized. Here, at night, the kitchen and bar glisten with a bright metallic resonance that speaks of good living in luxuriant surroundings.

This sleek kitchen and office combination was designed so typewriter, phone, and office materials would be close to the kitchen without being actually in it. Spare moments in the course of meal preparation—while you wait for water to boil or something to cook for five minutes—become "dead" time. Having office space nearby allows you to catch up on letter writing, bill paying, or list making. In this home, the entire area is unified with sedate grays and white. The hallway between the kitchen and office nook does not visually carve the area into two distinct places since floor material and color scheme draw both rooms together. The two vertical rows of glass bricks are clearly meant to diminish the effect the wall would have in separating the kitchen, hall, and office.

Young couples beginning to raise families buy or build a home after their apartment "stage," and they often design a family room in their new homes. It's usually just off the kitchen area, where they can easily slip into the evening rituals of reading, watching television, or playing games, and it's always close to the larder for late-night snacks. As in former times, the ideal family room includes a real hearth with real logs that burn with real fire and put out real heat. Of course, there are gas arrangements also, and they produce a kind of reality all their own.

The most recent development in home living that has revolutionized kitchen design is the move into loft apartments. Often incorporating as many square feet as a large sprawling home, the loft requires the judicious use of space and allocation of areas for various family and personal uses. In a loft, the kitchen can't always be completely hidden from the dining area, which in turn can't be concealed from the other living areas of the space. Even when visually distinct, there is frequently an audible overflow from one area to another. Kitchen decor in a

loft must complement the spaces to which it is a neighbor without clashing with the other moods and purposes. In effect, the kitchen must be a kitchen, but not look totally like a kitchen. It needs an ambiance of its own, but must also be akin to other places in the apartment.

Consequently, we find that the unique arrangements most worthy of note openly and cleverly mix various pastimes in one area, clustered around the basic features of the kitchen but still maintaining their own distinctiveness. A sleeping alcove, an entertain-

This executive's breakfast meetings might easily include eggs Benedict, a rather delightful strategy to assure that early morning meetings begin on time! In this glamorous office setting, important work and serious pleasures overlap; late dinners with a friend can be prepared while finishing up last-minute business of the day. In fact, as your gaze wanders around this room (even from a bird's-eye view overhead), you can easily overlook the black vinyl desk and other work-related furnishings; then the suite seems designed solely for elegant dinner parties. And yet, this is not a residential penthouse but an office. The striking color contrasts of black, pink, rose, and white are at once thoroughly feminine and thoroughly professional.

A simple tile platform raised from the hardwood floor in the main room designates the kitchen area proper and transforms this large area into functionally distinct spaces. The soft blue-green color tones that characterize the walls, ceiling, and cabinets form a gentle backdrop to the dark appliances and greenish black counter stools. Mirrors behind the sink and dark reflective panels on the appliances and counter create images of movement, shape, and color that enliven this sparsely decorated area. The unusual stools have handy footrests on them to make sitting more comfortable, and the vertebrae design is echoed in the lamp cords and the light fixtures themselves.

ment area, a home office, a media center—all these are just steps from the kitchen appliances.

Out of necessity, anyone trying to convert an extremely small space into a kitchen may stumble upon the unusual, if it be nothing more than arranging so many crucial appliances into a location that seems to defy their very existence. Luckily, kitchen manufacturers have developed miniature versions of standard-sized appliances for those tiny efficiency apartments and

those out-of-the-way nooks and crannies where you would like to add a sink, a grill, or a small fridge. In some older homes it makes more sense to convert the large kitchen into a dining room and place the actual kitchen facilities in a pantry or maid's room. Small galley kitchens like these can be easy and fun to work in if well designed, and the trade-off for getting more dining space is welcomed. The two- or three-kitchen home may become as common as the two- or three-

car garage, as kitchen areas are added to basement rathskellers where food and drink will be close to the poker game, pinochle contest, or PacMan tournament. Favorite locations for the second kitchen include the breezeway between the house and garage for more relaxed informal meals in the spring and summer months, the patio and poolside in the backyard.

*Y*ou owe yourself a personalized area in your home for your favorite hobbies

This loft kitchen is the ultimate in industrial design concept and yet small touches such as copper pots, a wooden table, and canvas strap chairs give it a homey feeling. The heavy metal frame overhead serves several purposes. In addition to creating a lowered ceiling effect, it holds the range hood and track lights; and it provides an ample supply of electrical outlets. The room is a typical blend of residential and commercial elements, reflected by the typical New York view from the window. The single eye-beam painted bright Chinese red effectively sections off the eating area in front from the stainelss-steel kitchen in the background.

and pastimes, and often the kitchen has all the equipment and facilities you need. In the case of hobbies and crafts that require water, a sink, and handy wash-up facilities, the kitchen is an ideal location. In a large roomy kitchen, one corner can accommodate your clay, paints, and ceramics. An unused pantry can become a dark room for photography. A sewing machine in a kitchen with a southern exposure will guarantee the bright light you need, and if it is placed near a window, may provide a pleasant view to relieve eyestrain resulting from close work. If you have small children at home, a play or crafts table in the kitchen lets them play freely without worrying about spills and messes in the one room made to withstand them. You can also supervise them while you're cooking the evening meal, cleaning up, or playing with your own arts and crafts.

*I*n the final analysis, the most appealing unusual arrangements in a kitchen are precisely those that suggest the play and good times that take place there, as well as the chores and tasks necessary to provide meals and clean up after. By its very nature the kitchen says "work" but it should also say "fun, happiness, and enjoyment," in terms other than food. Human beings have other appetites equally important if not as crucial as food. As more families indulge their personal needs and make space for them in or near the kitchen, the unusual settings and combinations that surprise us today may become traditional and ordinary tomorrow. For just as the human family evolves from generation to generation, all the while remaining curiously the same, so too will the kitchen undergo its own transformations.

This long sweeping view moves through three separate areas: the living room, the dining section, and the kitchen in the far back. The same beige dividers are used from room to room, which in turn match the cabinetry on the far wall and blend with the muted patterns and color of the sofa in the foreground. This is a simple but effective way to draw separate room elements together—one often overlooked by overly ambitious designers who are obsessed about decorating every square inch of room space. The conversation piece in the room is the fish tank built into the bookshelves, which entertains and relaxes family members with the dart-and-float activities of its inhabitants. A perfect feature for a home whose overall design is soothing and peaceful.

*A working fireplace is a welcome addition in any room of the house.
In the kitchen of this island summer home, it comes in handy during
off-season visits when chilly sea breezes blow around the house and
howl stiffly in the corners. The kitchen itself has a simple quarry-tile
floor and stark white walls, with decorative touches of food and
plants that reflect the bountiful summer months. The butcher block
type work island and open wood shelves create an airy, breezy
feel, as do the uncurtained windows and door. This is an easy kitchen
to maintain, containing no frivolous elements to take up time or
create unwanted chores. After all, the whole reason for being here is
outdoor fun. Who would want to be stuck inside caring for an
elaborate kitchen?*

Well-used and beloved cookbooks often become covered with stains because you unavoidably spill and splatter on the pages. You can probably even tell which recipes are a family's favorite, using the soiled pages as a corollary! But favorite cookbooks don't have to be splattered and smirched. Handy holders and racks can keep them open and propped up in plain view while you worry about ingredients. This cookbook rack is built right into the range hood, covered by attractive ceramic tiles, hand-painted with dainty sprigs of flora. The sloped hood tilts the book backward, high above splattering sauces but at an angle easy to read. Of course, you still have to remember to wipe your hands before you take it down.

Sometimes you don't need a complete kitchen for certain sections of your home or office, and yet one or two kitchen facilities would enhance the amenities of life were you to have them nearby. This has long been the motivation for including wet bars and extra refrigerators in a work or entertainment room. But slowly, the microwave oven is creeping in. Handy for warming up lunch or making a cup of tea, this little oven can fit in almost anywhere. It can be a handsome addition to a wall tastefully paneled with wooden cabinets and shelves, where a few ceramic utensils, some flowers, and a green plant make the niche particularly attractive.

In times of escalating real estate values, many people must opt for smaller kitchens when renting or buying a home. This New York penthouse has sacrificed a large kitchen for other amenities and consequently, the kitchen is short on counter space. But a clever designer minimized the problem by building in movable drawers that roll out to offer another work surface.

One of the primary human needs is warmth, and at some point in human history, fire was discovered as an important ingredient for food preparation. Since then, inventors have concocted various methods to bring raw food and fire together to produce the desired menu. Eventually it was learned that an actual flame was not necessary—heat was. And so in our own century we have seen the old-fashioned woodstove and the gas range replaced by electric stoves and microwave appliances, both of which cook a meal without a flame. Even in this kitchen where a love of the past is so meticulously expressed, the "fireless" ovens have found a niche.

The benefit of placing a wet bar and a small refrigerator outside the main kitchen can be seen here. The host or hostess can serve drinks and refreshments to guests before dinner while the cook tends to last-minute details in the kitchen. Parties always seem to center in or near the kitchen, because that's where the beverages are, so why not install a satellite station just outside the kitchen to attract thirsty friends and leave the kitchen uncrowded? A key element to successful kitchen layout is control of traffic flow. Here, the tactic is to divert traffic altogether by a lush ambush of cocktails and hors d'oeuvres right outside the kitchen door.

7

Styles and Motifs

Choosing a style or motif for a kitchen is often analogous to selecting a new wardrobe. We decide on the "look" we hope will impress others; frequently, the real "us" is camouflaged behind a fashion trend that is not completely true to our own identity. So too, a kitchen may appear on the surface to be high-tech or Mexican or 1940s when, in reality, it is something quite different. This is not the case with this New Jersey kitchen, however. No artificial beams or prematurely aged bricks have been added; this is truly an old farmhouse. It has been renovated for modern living but retains the original structure and architectural elements of the old country kitchen it is. Judging by its look of solidity, this cozy room will continue to celebrate country things for many years to come.

Every style makes a statement, and every room announces the thoughts and feelings of the people who use it. Like an outer mirror, each room reflects the interior dreams and aspirations of its owner in the colors, lines, themes, and patterns that distinguish it, for interior designs seldom deceive. When studied closely they are more than masks that hide the values and sentiments of the people who inhabit them. Even in their attempted deceptions, they record and capture the consciousness of the human personalities that created them. Few rooms are merely neutral settings. They are active, although silent, participants in our external lives as well as in our imaginations. So much human life is lived in the kitchen, so many major and minor dramas are played out around its table, that the elements of style do indeed become the elements of emotion, thought, and feeling there. Images of the kitchens we have known return to us throughout our lives and remain preserved as some of our most important memories.

Not until the eighteenth century did English homes begin to include a specific room for dining. Prior to that, the custom was to eat in whatever room satisfied the whimsy of the day. And when the meal was concluded, the servants whisked the dirty dishes out to the far-removed kitchen where they were washed and dried for the next meal. In America the practice of locating the kitchen on a separate floor, usually below the dining room, persisted well into the twentieth century among the upper middle classes. Clearly the indoor kitchen as a standard room awaited breakthroughs in technology so that house construction could include indoor plumbing for water and other safety measures to ac-commodate the peculiar needs of the household kitchen.

The kitchen as a family room that included the central hearth—or hearth substitute—was really pioneered by middle and lower middle class families who could not afford spacious homes with separate cooking and dining areas. For them, the preparing and eating of meals took place in one large room, usually with an appliance on each wall, a solid bulky table in the middle, and black and white checkerboard tiles or linoleum on the floor. It wasn't designed to save steps nor for the most efficient arrangement of appliances, but it was the center of family life. In the winter, the old stove even provided heat for drying laundry, and in the hot summers the ice box, literally a box with a cake of ice in it, could be raided with an ice pick for a cold sliver to suck on while the lemons were being squeezed for lemonade.

After World War II, kitchen decor became sterile and dull, as efficiency reigned even to the point of excluding taste and style. The trend was to capitalize on the new labor-saving conveniences and create an environment for them and nothing else—at least nothing that would counteract the desire for sleek, practical, and efficient management of meals. With the appliance boom in the 1960s and 1970s, many kitchens virtually became Disneylands of gadgetry. At this stage even the most modern appliances were still large and cumbersome, chrome-colored, shiny, or white. But in the last ten years or so, technological design has made appliances more harmonious, quieter, and they are now available in softer colors that are more tasteful and pleasing. The kitchen itself has developed into a warmer, cozier, and more luxurious place where aesthetic considerations

Trompe l'oeil is a style that makes no excuses for deception. In fact, its ability to create illusion is what makes it so appealing and what determines its appropriateness. Under the mastery of a skilled artist, a plain two-dimensional wall can disappear into sweeping landscapes, billowing clouds, intricate woodwork, or, as seen here, the homey feel of a well-stocked pantry. Look closely to discover what's edible and what's not, for the items behind the basket of onions and the clay urn are not up for grabs—neither are the shelves they're sitting on. It's all painted. Even the rich wood grain in the cabinetry, wall, and door came from the artist's palette not a forest. And the quaintly chipped flagstone floor? It's as easy to care for as vinyl.

This kitchen has been beautifully re-created by professional restorationists who specialize in eighteenth-century styles. Rural to the smallest detail, even the view from this hilltop dwelling has the timeless stillness that suggests country living during almost any century. The rough-hewn beams overhead are ideal for hanging baskets, an old-fashioned colander, and other kitchen utensils made from materials of an earlier day. In this home the divider between kitchen and eating area is a bare half wall, simple wooden planks nailed to the support pillars. The shaggy, unfinished surfaces of the walls and ceiling contrast nicely with the polished countertops and the antique green of the cabinets and trim.

are as important as utilitarian ones. In fact, the kitchen in the last few years has become a room that is as challenging and fun to decorate as any other room of the house. Style is a major category on the design menu and many selections are available. We are fortunate to live at the end of so many eras, for from each of them we can glean styles and motifs, which, when judiciously mated or mixed, can create a kitchen environment that is uniquely and distinctly our own.

A perennially favorite style dates back to the early farm kitchen that played such an important role in the growing and processing of food. Virtually a national heritage, the country kitchen pleases almost everyone's taste. With exposed beams, honest open shelves, and a wealth of wood that lends a warm and secure feeling to the room, the country kitchen can look bustling and busy and still retain a clean and stylish aura. It never has that don't-touch-me-I'm-clean look even when it is spotless. The country style invites activity and commotion. You feel at home in it whatever you do. You can relax.

At the opposite end of the spectrum is the high-tech kitchen that has an industrial appearance bringing to mind rigid health codes and undeviating inspectors. Utilizing commercial appliances wherever possible, the sleek, spic-and-span kitchen demands that it have a sterile look, equating sterility with hygiene. It is easy to maintain because the furnishings are hardy and durable and designed to meet high standards of cleanliness. Although the high-tech design satisfies a certain taste, and can blend harmoniously with the rest of the home, it is not as warm, comforting, and inviting as other styles.

Another favorite from the American past is the colonial kitchen with its rows of pewter mugs and plates standing at patriotic attention on a heavy mantelpiece over a fireplace, and baskets hanging from the ceiling beams. Chippendale cabinets proudly display a fine collection of porcelain and the dining area is furnished with colonial-style table and chairs surrounded by eighteenth-century patterned wallpaper. In these kitchens, it's easy to understand how patriotism came to be equated with motherhood and apple pies.

The Shaker kitchen combines both the creativity of yesteryear with the minimalist values of today. The ladder-back chairs and the clean, unadorned lines of its woodwork are easy to care for and lend an austere though friendly quality to the kitchen. Here you can have the warmth and softness of wood molded by conscientious craftspeople with the ease and efficiency of modern maintenance techniques. A style that might be called "minimalist traditional," the Shaker kitchen satisfies the aesthetic tension of many people who wish to retain the distinctive charm of the past but incorporate it into the simplicity desired in a no-frills kitchen that is easy to care for.

For the modernist who wants simply the basics, "contemporary minimalism" is the answer. Even in color and pattern, the minimalist kitchen tends to be monotoned, often in white or off-white, with perhaps a few splashes of some contrasting tone; if there are any decorative touches, they are simple and spare, one plant perhaps, and a large poster. The eye has little to distract it, and the mind is left to concentrate on preparing the meal.

Trompe l'oeil is a natural for kitchens where illusion is necessary to

A carnival spirit pervades this kitchen where suggestions of a harlequin are seen in the black-and-white-tiled backsplash and the illusive cabinet doors that alternate between wood and dark glass. Even the white countertop on the island in the middle seems to be precariously balanced. A touch of the magician, the acrobatic dexterity of the juggler, the good humor of the clown, and the command of the ringmaster can be felt in this circular room built from black and white cubes stacked on top each other.

create diversity amid large clunky appliances. Utilizing illusionistic art, the kitchen designer can create the impression of far-off vistas, classical ruins, or any theatrical ambiance the owner desires. Especially important in small kitchens where the illusion of space is needed, the *trompe l'oeil* decor can extend the room, if only in the mind's eye, and seem to expand the area. It may even include whimsical notes, light fantasies, or humorous statements to enliven the often monotonous chores that are unavoidable. If nothing more, *trompe l'oeil* can create the impression of contrasting textures, such as wood, marble, or tile, where there is really only plaster or wallboard.

Japanese-style techniques have become extremely popular in loft apartments where various spaces must be created for the different functions of the home. Using simple rice paper or bamboo partitions, the dining area can be quickly and neatly separated from the kitchen itself. If you want to minimize the amount of space used for the kitchen, a low Japanese table with pillows instead of chairs, plus a wok or tableside grill, will produce an informal ambiance that can be easily changed when the area is needed for some other activity. A Japanese lantern and Oriental place settings will complete the touch of the Far East.

*A 1940s aura settles down in this kitchen/living room combination.
The wallpaper swirls with billowing lines and offers a delicate
backdrop to larger swaths of color—black floor, white armchairs,
and the solid white walls and cabinets of the kitchen itself. Judicious
touches of red highlight the black-and-white motif, playfully
interchanging the two colors—white stools against the black counter,
and black chairs around the clear glass table by the door.*

The desert Southwest contributes many ideas for kitchen decor. Clean, unadorned adobe walls seem to belong in a kitchen where brightness and cleanliness are desired. Indian, Mexican, and Spanish motifs abound for trim, tile, and other decorative touches. It is a spare look that fits our present sensibility about how a kitchen should look. This motif speaks of the open hearth and the fast-paced, outdoor lifestyle popularized in the

Southwest and adapted by so many other parts of the country, just as Mexican traditional cooking has been adopted by places farther north. Like the extended families that lived in them, the Spanish-Indian style kitchens exude a warmth and friendliness associated with corn cakes and large pots of aromatic stew.

Whether you design your kitchen for a growing family or for yourself alone, this all-important room deserves the

attention comparable to the essential needs it helps to fill in your life. Its utilitarian functions are only part of the message behind it, for it is in the kitchen that the physical needs of the human being are extended to higher values. Love, friendship, and sharing are as much a part of meals as meat and potatoes. The challenge for you is to create the atmosphere that will help to raise their hopes and aspirations beyond the kitchen.

The rock music writer who designed this 1950s kitchen has successfully captured the feel of the old soda fountain diner where so many people spent idle hours of their adolescence. Before school, during school, and after school, booths like this one were packed with teenagers discussing the merits of their favorite rock-'n'-roll singers whose hit tunes could be played for just a nickel on the flip jukebox in each booth. The vinyl tile floor has a faint wisp of nostalgia, with its tail-fin automobile and rocket ship that would soon take us into space and another age—far beyond the nickel jukebox.

Another 1950s-era kitchen—antiseptically clean, unpretentious, strictly utilitarian. The three color tones—all on the same end of the color spectrum—were considered de rigeur for kitchen interiors. To paraphrase Henry Ford, for a kitchen, any color is all right so long as it's yellow—or some close variation of it. Today, looking back at these colorful though austere kitchens, their exuberant simplicity is striking as a somewhat welcome alternative to the lavishness, that many contemporary kitchen designers have popularized in recent years. They are helpful reminders that bring us back to a basic value: a kitchen's real worth depends on how well it allows a talented cook to prepare delicious meals, not on how it mesmerizes us by its theme or style.

The latest utilitarian look comes from Italy, but it is one that manages to break away from the stark empty feeling of many kitchens designed for efficiency rather than aesthetics. This kitchen says "cute" without being saccharine sweet. In fact, its sparse, diminutive style speaks of necessity rather than conceit. Engineered to accommodate a small area such as this corner, the designer has incorporated the essential cooking equipment and two sinks into a space which would be unusable for more ambitious kitchen facilities. The dainty peppermint wallpaper works as a foil to enlarge the appliances and utensils, even drawing attention to the miniature stools, which in this scheme play a role larger than their size.

This colorful kitchen, also Italian, demonstrates yet another way the no-frills design of a small space can handle cooking and eating activities without a total kitchen look. In fact, at first glance there isn't very much that looks kitchenish about this setting. Like a doll's house, the area has a preciousness to it that is not disconcerting. Despite the carefully arranged accessories in a minimum amount of storage space, the room looks like it would be easy to live and work in. With major appliances along another wall, this corner would become a cheerful haven for a tranquil cup of coffee or a brief pause in the course of a busy day.

A Japanese motif will appeal to those who have a penchant for the minimalist look but who also shy away from the starkly utilitarian look of so many modern designs. The warm bamboo fronts on these cabinets give this kitchen a pleasant uniformity typical of Japanese interior design. This strategy eliminates extraneous adornments and extravagant decorative touches that require each nook and corner to have a character of its own. The clean empty panels are meant to retain their wholeness. The large window above the sink lets the natural sunlight in, but is harmonized with the rest of the room by the individual pane design. Only a few simple fans, trays, a bonzai plant, and a couple blossoms are needed to break up the continuous bamboo color trimmed in black.

Here is another attractive way to handle an L-shaped kitchen. One end—down front and to the left—is arranged for the heavy-duty working area; the other end—receding into the background—is designed primarily for cabinetry, storage, and a salad preparation counter with small sink and a few spices and herbal ingredients. The white marble counters give this area a bright, clean, healthy look as they trim the dark Chinese red cabinetry. The sheer bulk of the cabinets counterbalances the massive industrial stove on the right. Notice the spare use of ceramic tile that designates the work areas proper, and note how the stepped effect of the tile moves out of the kitchen and into other rooms of the house. The countertops themselves make a saw-toothed exit in the far left.

You might expect only exotic meals of venison and wild boar to be served in this exciting kitchen that bursts with animal life and suggests shaded groves where trekkers might pause while big game hunting. The deep jungle-green walls are trimmed with an unfinished blond wood that resembles rough constructions built as overnight camps for safari-goers. The room is decorated with stark white bestiary sculptures that include deer, moose antlers, ducks, swan, and fish— a truly whimsical assortment of wildlife to titillate the imagination between the papaya appetizer and ibex consommé.

Eating in this decorative corner is an adventure in fantasy. The naturescape on the wall is a lavish blend of lush green vegetation and ornately civilized detail. So, too, is the room, encapsulated in a vibrating green-and-white checkerboard wallpaper that breathes a quiet bustle. You would imagine that only perky meals seasoned with mentally alert conversation would be served here. The room itself is an alluring conversation piece, centered around the heavy ceramic table base that suggests a white tree trunk entwined by vines. It is a fitting companion to the egg-shaped vegetable pods in the corner. The complimentary touch of pink-and-white striped cushions and napkins completes the minty decor that dominates the room.

This utilitarian kitchen proves that the practical can have a crisp elegance of its own. The bright room is not cluttered with color, nor is it a difficult room to clean, even after the largest dinner party. There is a liquid stillness to this kitchen, possibly effected by the sharp, almost invisible mirrors that panel the refrigerator door and the backsplash behind the sink, creating an illusion of depth that defies our sense of geography. The extraordinarily adaptable pentagonal island could easily seat from two to five in a three-quarter round arrangement. Its skewed sides offset the parallel and perpendicular lines of the room. Another masterful touch that perfects the hygienic quality of this kitchen is the continuation of the white ceramic floor tiles on the countertop.

The concentric squares of the marquee-style light track on this black ceiling offer a burst of light and a stroke of symmetry to a polysided, strangely angular room. The crinkled vinyl tile floor provides a softness to the hard straight lines and insistent color combination. As in other basically black and white kitchens, bold use of bright red brings an exciting erotic accent. The striking upward thrust of the wide-based stools creates a sense of liftoff, raising the optical center of the room. More so than in other kitchens of similar design, this one capitalizes on the absence of handles, knobs, and other cabinetry hardware, giving the room a clean, almost empty feel.

There is an almost illusive division between the kitchen and the living room in this home, and yet the division is there. The unusual and distinctive furniture sets the two rooms apart, yet the smoked-blue furnishings tell us that these rooms are very compatible. The lack of trim, the curved hard edges, and the matte finish produce a soft, gentle aura, further stated in the muted pink cushions and pillows. The oddly shaped range hood over the working and dining counter descends with a forthright authority. The unfinished edge of the work area is designated by the spillover effect of floor tiles. The final product is an easy space in which to work and live, where activities flow from one room to another.

Here, subtle splashes of pink carry a visitor's gaze around the room from one area to another. The overstuffed easy chair and floor lamp allow reading and conversation to take place only a few steps from the kitchen. The mushroom-shaped shade is a variation on the bell-shaped fixtures over the dining table. The black grate ceiling relaxes into an oriental trellis behind the table that effectively sections off the major work area from the cabinet and storage panel.

*Finally we return to this dark, pensive kitchen excitingly furnished
with the assertive stainless steel of industrial appliances. This daring
design of dark and light contrasts is reminiscent of the full scope of
kitchen styles—from the all-white, sunny, and open kitchen that
bustles with human voices to kitchens like the one above where
preparing a meal is an act of meditation. This is a room made of
concentrations—the black cupboards are solid and continuous; the
steel appliances are sturdy and imposing; even the haphazard red
details leap out in their intensity. Here is the kitchen for the chef who
enjoys solitude and a minimum of distractions, a kitchen that
reminds us that the culinary art begins in the deep desires of the human
mind and heart, and ends in companionship and the sharing of food.*

Sources/
Useful Addresses

UNITED STATES

General

AMERICAN GAS ASSOCIATION
1515 Wilson Boulevard
Arlington, VA 22209

AMERICAN INSTITUTE OF ARCHITECTS
1735 New York Avenue, NW
Washington, DC 20006

AMERICAN INSTITUTE OF KITCHEN
DEALERS
114 Main Street
Hackettstown, NJ 07804

THE ELECTRIFICATION COUNCIL
90 Park Avenue
New York, NY 10016

NATIONAL ELECTRICAL MANUFACTURERS
ASSOCIATION
115 East 44th Street
New York, NY 10017

NATIONAL HOUSEWARES
MANUFACTURERS ASSOCIATION
1130 Merchandise Mart
Chicago, IL 60654

NATIONAL WOODWORK MANUFACTURERS
ASSOCIATION
400 West Madison Street
Chicago, IL 60606

Floors, Walls, and Ceiling Materials

AGENCY TILES INC.
499 Old Nyack Turnpike
Spring Valley, NY 10977

AMERICAN OLEAN TILE CO.
1000 Cannon Avenue
Landsdale, PA 19446

AMTICO FLOORING DIVISION
American Biltrite Inc.
Amtico Square
Trenton, NJ 98607

ARKANSAS OAK FLOORING CO.
Pine Bluff, AR 71601

ARMSTRONG CORK CO.
Liberty and Charlotte
Lancaster, PA 17604

BINSWANGER MIRROR CO.
1355 Lynnfield Road
Memphis, TN 38117

E.L. BRUCE CO. INC.
P.O. Box 16902
Memphis, TN 38116

CHAMPION BUILDING PRODUCTS
CHAMPION INTERNATIONAL CORP.
1 Landmark Square
Stamford, CT 06921

CHINA SEAS INC.
149 East 72nd Street
New York, NY 10021

COHAMA DECORATIVE FABRICS
1280 North Grant Avenue
Columbus, OH 43216

CONGOLEUM INDUSTRIES INC.
195 Belgrove Drive
Kearny, NJ 07032

CORK PRODUCTS CO. INC.
250 Park Avenue South
New York, NY 10003

COUNTRY FLOORS INC.
300 East 61st Street
New York, NY 10021

CROWN INDUSTRIES
DIVISION LUDLOW CORP.
2100 Commerce Drive
Fremont, OH 43420

CROWN WALLCOVERING CORP.
979 Third Avenue
New York, NY 10022

DESIGNERS TILE INTERNATIONAL
6812 SW 81st Street
Miami, FL 33143

DURAWALL INC.
10 Market Street
Kenilworth, NJ 07033

FORMICA CORP.
120 East Fourth Street
Cincinnati, OH 45202

FRANCISCAN FABRICS INC.
938 Harrison Street
San Francisco, CA 94107

GEORGIA MARBLE CO.
Cumberland Parkway, NW
Atlanta, GA 30339

GEORGIA PACIFIC CORP.
900 SW Fifth Avenue
Portland, OR 97204

B.F. GOODRICH
GENERAL PRODUCTS CO.
500 Main Street
Akron, OH 44318

HARRIS HARDWOOD CO. INC.
Roanoke, VA 24015

HASTINGS TILE
964 Third Avenue
New York, NY 10022

HOUSE OF CERAMICS INC.
17 Putnam Avenue
Port Chester, NY 10573

ITALIAN MARBLE INDUSTRIES
228 Park Avenue South
New York, NY 10003

ITALIAN TILE CENTER
499 Park Avenue
New York, NY 10022

KENTILES FLOORS INC.
58 Second Avenue
Brooklyn, NY 11215

MANNINGTON
P.O. Box 30
Salem, NJ 08079

MEMPHIS HARDWOOD FLOORING CO.
1551 Thomas
Memphis, TN 38107

MID-STATE TILE CO.
P.O. Box 627
Lexington, NC 27292

MOHAWK CARPET
919 Third Avenue
New York, NY 10022

MONARCH CARPET MILLS
5025 New Peachtree Road
Chamblee, GA 30341

NATIONAL FLOOR PRODUCTS CO. INC.
P.O. Box 354-A
Florence, AL 35630

R.C. OWEN CO.
Lafayette Road
Hopkinsville, KY 42240

PEMAQUID FLOORCLOTHS
Pemaquid, ME 04558

SIGNATURE FLOORS INC.
979 Third Avenue
New York, NY 10022

STARK CERAMICS INC.
P.O. Box 8880
Canton, OH 44711

U.S. CERAMIC TILE CO.
1375 Raff Road NW
Canton, OH 44710

U.S. GYPSUM CO.
101 South Wacker Drive
Chicago, IL 60606

VERMONT MARBLE CO.
61 Main Street
Proctor, VT 05765

VIKING CARPETS INC.
10 West 33rd Street
New York, NY 10001

VIP FINE MARBLE INC.
210 Lawrence Avenue
Staten Island, NY 10310

Doors and Windows

CREATIVE WOODWORKING CO.
1370 Ralph Avenue
Brooklyn, NY 11236

GEORGIA PACIFIC CORP.
900 SW Fifth Avenue
Portland, OR 97204

LOUVERDRAPE INC.
1100 Colorado Avenue
Santa Monica, CA 90401

MODERN PARTITIONS
Division Trendway Corp.
P.O. Box 728
Holland, MI 49423

PINECREST INC.
2118 Blaisdell Avenue South
Minneapolis, MN 55404

ONE TOUCH OF GLAMOUR INC.
6130 North Broadway
Chicago, IL 60660

VAUGHAN WALLS INC.
11681 San Vicente Boulevard
Los Angeles, CA 90049

VENETIAN BLIND COUNCIL
P.O. Box 670
East Orange, NJ 07018

WINDOW SHADE MANUFACTURERS
ASSOC.
Executive Plaza
1211 West 22nd Street
Oak Brook, IL 60521

WOODWORK CORP. OF AMERICA
1432 West 21st Street
Chicago, IL 60608

Major Appliances

ABBAKA TRADE CO.
SCANDINAVIAN IMPORTS
P.O. Box 3435
San Francisco, CA 94119

ACME NATIONAL REFRIGERATOR CO.
10-26 Hazen Street
Astoria, NY 11105

ADMIRAL CORPORATION
1701 East Woodfield Road
Schaumberg, IL 60172

AMANA REFRIGERATION INC.
Amana, IA 52204

BAKERS PRIDE OVEN CO.
1641 East 233rd Street
Bronx, NY 10466

CERVITOR KITCHENS INC.
1500-1516 Santa Anita
El Monte, CA 91733

FARBERWARE
100 Electra Lane
Yonkers, NY 10704

FRIGIDAIRE DIVISION, GMC
300 Taylor Street
Dayton, OH 45442

GENERAL ELECTRIC CO.
APPLIANCE DIVISION
Appliance Park
Louisville, KY 40225

GIBSON APPLIANCE CORP.
Gibson Appliance Center
1401 Van Deinse Road
Greenville, MI 48838

HOOVER CO.
101 East Maple Street
North Canton, OH 44720

HOTPOINT CONTRACT SALES
GENERAL ELECTRIC CO.
Appliance Park
Louisville, KY 40225

HOYT MANUFACTURING CORP.
100 Forge Road
Westport, MA 02790

KENMORE
SEARS, ROEBUCK, AND CO.
Sears Tower
Chicago, IL 60684

KITCHENAID
Hobart Corp.
Troy, OH 45374

KICH-N-VENT
HOME METAL PRODUCTS CO.
750 Central Expressway
Plano, TX 75074

KING REFRIGERATOR CORP.
76-02 Woodhaven Boulevard
Glendale, NY 11227

LITTON MICROWAVE COOKING PRODUCTS
1405 Xenium Lane
Minneapolis, MN 55441

THE MAYTAG CO.
403 North Fourth Street
Newton, IA 50208

MODERN MAID DIVISION
McGRAW-EDISON CO.
P.O. Box 1111
Chattanooga, TN 37401

MONARCH KITCHEN APPLIANCE CO.
715 North Spring Street
Beaver Dam, WI 53196

NORGE CO.
410 East Maple Street
Herrin, IL 62948

ROYAL CHEF DIVISION
GRAY AND DUDLEY CO.
2300 Clifton Road
Nashville, TN 37209

SANYO ELECTRICAL INC.
APPLIANCE DIVISION
51 Joseph Street
Moonachie, NJ 07074

SHARP ELECTRONICS CORP.
10 Keystone Place
Paramus, NJ 07652

SPEED QUEEN DIVISION
McGRAW-EDISON CO.
Ripon, WI 54071

SUB-ZERO FREEZER CO. INC.
P.O. Box 4130
Madison, WI 53711

SUNRAY STOVE CO.
DIVISION GLENWOOD RANGE CO.
435 Park Avenue
Delaware, OH 43015

TAPPAN CO.
Tappan Park
P.O. Box 606
Mansfield, OH 44901

THERMADOR/WASTE KING
5119 District Boulevard
Los Angeles, CA 90040

UNITED REFRIGERATOR CO.
P.O. Box 247
Hudson, WI 54016

WHIRLPOOL CORP.
Administrative Center
Benton Harbor, MI 49022

WHITE-WESTINGHOUSE CORP.
930 Fort Duquesne Boulevard
Pittsburgh, PA 15222

Sinks

AMERICAN BRASS MFG. CO.
5000 Superior Avenue
Cleveland, OH 44103

AMERICAN STANDARD INC.
P.O. Box 2003
New Brunswick, NJ 08903

ARUNDALE INC.
1173 Reco Avenue
St. Louis, MO 63126

CONSUMER PRODUCTS
P.O. Box 171231
Memphis, TN 38117

CROWN-NATIONAL CO.
266 Eisenhower Lane
Lombard, IL 60148

FAUCET-QUEENS INC.
1741 West Belmont Avenue
Chicago, IL 60657

FEDERAL STAINLESS SINK
UNARCO INDUSTRIES
P.O. Box 429
Paris, IL 61944

HALSEY TAYLOR CO.
1554 Thomas Road SE
Warren, OH 44481

INDIANA BRASS CO. INC.
P.O. Box 367
Frankfort, IN 46041

IN-SINK-ERATOR
DIVISION EMERSON ELECTRIC CO.
4700 21st Street
Racine, WI 53406

KOHLER CO.
Kohler, WI 53044

L&M CULTURED MARBLE CO.
6433 West 99th Street
Chicago Ridge, IL 60415

LEGION STAINLESS SINK CORP.
21-07 40th Avenue
Long Island City, NY 11101

MAGIC CHEF INC.
740 King Edward Avenue
Cleveland, TN 37311

THE MAYTAG CO.
403 North Fourth Street
Newton, IA 50208

MARBLETEK CORP.
44 Lochdale Road
Roslindale, MA 02131

MICHIGAN BRASS CO.
500 South Water Street
Grand Haven, MI 49417

MILWAUKEE FAUCETS INC.
4250 North 124th Street
Milwaukee, WI 53222

MOLDED MARBLE PRODUCTS
DIVISION LIPPERT CORP.
P.O. Box 219
Menomonee Falls, WI 53051

NEPTUNE LIFETIME SUITES
1801 West 1912 Street
Broadview, IL 60153

THE REVERE SINK CORP.
44 Coffin Avenue
New Beford, MA 02746

ROBINSON EXPORT-IMPORT CORP.
6732 Industrial Road
Springfield, VA 22151

STAINLESS STEEL SINK INC.
300 Fay Avenue
P.O. Box 296
Addison, IL 60101

THE STERLING SINK CO.
123 Forbes Road
P.O. Box 2334
Gastonia, NC 28052

TAPPAN APPLIANCE DIVISION
Tappan Park
Mansfield, OH 44901

TOWN CRAFT VANITIES
15-32 127th Street
College Point, NY 11356

WASTE KING
DIVISION NORRIS INDUSTRIES
5119 District Boulevard
Los Angeles, CA 90040

WHIRLPOOL CORP.
Administrative Center
Benton Harbor, MI 49022

Small Appliances/Accessories

CUISINARTS INC.
P.O. Box 353
Greenwich, CT 06830

DYNAMICS CORP. OF AMERICA
Route 44
New Hartford, CT 06057

FARBERWARE
DIVISION LCA CORP.
100 Electra Lane
Yonkers, NY 10704

GENERAL ELECTRIC CO.
HOUSEWARES DIVISION
1285 Boston Avenue
Bridgeport, CT 06610

INTERNATIONAL REGISTER CO.
4700 West Montrose Avenue
Chicago, IL 60641

KITCHENAID
Hobart Corp.
Troy, OH 45374

MAGIC MILL
DIVISION STRATFORD SQUIRE
INTERNATIONAL
235 West Second Street
Salt Lake City, UT 84101

RONSON CORP.
1 Ronson Road
Ogletown, DE 19702

SALTON INC.
1260 Zerega Avenue
Bronx, NY 10462

SUNBEAM CORP.
5400 West Roosevelt Road
Chicago, IL 60650

Furniture

CHAIRCRAFT INC.
P.O. Box 2627
Hickory, NC 28601

JAMES DAVID
128 Weldon Parkway
Maryland Heights, MO 63043

DIN-A-CO.
500 South Hicks Road
Palatine, IL 60067

EVER-READY APPLIANCE MFG.
5727 West Park
St. Louis, MO 63110

HARRY LEVITZ CO. INC.
230 Fifth Avenue
New York, NY 10001

KITCHEN NOOKS INC.
2575 Park Road
Hallandale, FL 33009

SAMSONITE CORP.
11200 East 45th Avenue
Denver, CO 80217

SHAMROCK INDUSTRIES INC.
1010 Lydnale Avenue North
Minneapolis, MN 55411

STYLE TREND DINING NOOKS
B.L. BRINKLEY CO.
24710 Westmoreland Drive
Farmington, MI 48024

TRI-ART BREAKFAST NOOKS
500 Sunrise Highway
Rockville Center, NY 11570

Lighting

AMERICAN HOME LIGHTING INSTITUTE
230 North Michigan Avenue
Chicago, IL 60601

FLUORESCENT LIGHTING ASSOCIATION
101 Park Avenue
New York, NY 10017

GENERAL ELECTRIC CO.
Nela Park
Cleveland, OH 44112

GTE SYLVANIA INC.
1 Stamford Forum
Stamford, CT 06904

HOUSE OF RAND
681 Main Street
Belleville, NJ 07109

INCANDESCENT LAMP MANUFACTURERS
ASSOC.
760 South 13th Street
Newark, NY 07103

LIGHTOLIER INDUSTRIES
346 Claremont Avenue
Jersey City, NJ 07305

NUTONE HOUSING PRODUCTS
Madison and Red Bank Roads
Cincinnati, OH 45227

PANASONIC SPECIAL PRODUCTS DIVISION
200 Park Avenue
Pan American Building
New York, NY 10017

SUNRAY LIGHTING CO.
4228 Sepulveda Boulevard
Culver City, CA 90230

TELEDYNE BIG BEAM
292 East Prairie Street
Crystal Lake, IL 60014

WHITE-WESTINGHOUSE ELECTRIC CORP.
INTERIOR LIGHTING DIVISION
U.S. Highway 61 South
P.O. Box 824
Vicksburg, MO 39181

Cabinetry/Storage

Adelphi Kitchens
3000 Penn Avenue
West Lawn, PA 19609

AMERICAN CABINET CORP.
P.O. Box 1326
Dublin, GA 31021

ALLMILMO (USA)
70 Clinton Road
Fairfield, NJ 07006

BIRCHCRAFT KITCHENS
1612 Thorn Street
Reading, PA 19601

CABINETWORKS
9424 Roosevelt Way NE
Seattle, WA 98115

CONTINENTAL KITCHENS INC.
Building 26
Spokane Industrial Park
Spokane, WA 99216

COUNTRY KRAFT KITCHENS INC.
Newmanstown, PA 17173

CRAFT MAID CUSTOM KITCHENS INC.
P.O. Box 4026
Reading, PA 19606

CREATIVE CABINETS INC.
3215 North Pan Am Expressway
San Antonio, TX 78220

CROWN KITCHEN CABINET CORP.
9200 Atlantic Avenue
Ozone Park, NY 11416

CUSTOM FURNITURE AND CABINETS
Route 5, Box 892
Post Falls, ID 83854

DURA CRAFT KITCHENS
A DIVISION OF L&M MFG. CO.
110 West Oak Street
Gillespie, IL 62033

DURA MAID INDUSTRIES INC.
Architectural Material Center
101 Park Avenue
New York, NY 10017

HÄFELE AMERICA CO.
P.O. Box 1590
High Point, NC 27261

HERITAGE CABINETS INC.
348 Broad Street
Fitchburg, MA 01420

KITCHEN CONCEPTS INC.
3601 Princeton NE
Albuquerque, NM 87107

IMPERIAL CABINET CO. INC.
P.O. Box 427
Gaston, IN 47342

KELLER KITCHEN CABINETS
SOUTHERN CORP.
P.O. Box 1089
Deland, FL 32720

KEMPER
DIVISION OF THE TAPPAN CO.
701 South North Street
Richmond, IN 47374

MARYLAND MAID KITCHENS
DIVISION OF COLONIAL HARDWOOD
FLOORING
227 East Washington Street
Hagerstown, MD 21740

MEDALLION KITCHENS INC.
810 First Street South
Hopkins, MN 55343

MILLER MAID CABINETS INC.
4805 Hardegon Road
Indianapolis, IN 46227

MOTHER HUBBARD'S CUPBOARDS
1835 Dual Highway
Hagerstown, MD 21740

NORTH AMERICAN CABINET CORP.
701 South Grove
Marshall, TX 76570

NORTH VALLEY PLASTICS INC.
4650 Catepillar Road
Redding, CA 96001

NORTHERN KITCHENS
Rib Lake, WI 54470

OLDE TOWNE CUPBOARDS CORP.
Souderton, PA 18964

PIONEER CRAFTSMAN INC.
333 North Third Street
Reading, PA 19601

POGGENPOHL
222 Cedar Lane
Teaneck, NJ 07666

PRESTIGE CABINET CORP. OF AMERICA
29 Rider Place
Freeport, NY 11520

PRESTIGE PRODUCTS INC.
P.O. Box 314
Twin Rivers Industrial Park
Neodasha, KS 66757

QUAKER MAID
Route 61
Leesport, PA 19533

REGAL CABINET INC.
315 Holland Sylvania
Toledo, OH 43615

RIVIERA PRODUCTS
DIVISION OF EVANS PRODUCTS CO.
1960 Seneca Road
St. Paul, MN 55122

ST. CHARLES MFG. CO.
1611 East Main Street
St. Charles, IL 60174

SIEMATIC USA
7206 Georgetown Road
Santa Barbara, CA 93117

SOUTHWESTERN CABINET CO.
P.O. Box 889
Dothan, AL 36301

SUNEARTH CABINETWORKS
Spring House Village Center
Spring House, PA 19477

SUPERIOR WOOD WORK INC.
7157 Dale Road
El Paso, TX 79915

TRIANGLE PACIFIC CABINET CORP.
4255 LBJ Freeway
Dallas, TX 75234

UNITED CABINET DIVISION
BEATRICE FOODS CO.
P.O. Box 420
Jasper, IN 47546

VALLEY KITCHENS INC.
123 West Main Street
Lebanon, OH 45036

WILSONART
600 General Bruce Drive
Temple, TX 76501

Worktops

BUTCHERBLOCK
1864 Massachusetts Avenue
Cambridge, MA 02140

DURA-BEAUTY
CONSOWELD CORP.
700 Durabeauty Lane
Wisconsin Rapids, WI 54494

E.I. DUPONT DE NUMOURS & CO.
Tatnall Building
Products Information Section
Wilmington, DE 19898

FORMICA CORPORATION
120 East Fourth Street
Cincinnati, OH 45202

CANADA

Certified Kitchen Designers

GARY BISHOP, CKD
MERIT KITCHEN CENTRE
2401 Burrard Street
Vancouver, British Columbia

FRED BOWMEISTER, CKD
DREGER'S KITCHEN CORNER
10442 82nd Avenue
Edmonton, Alberta

KEN CASSIN, CKD
2101 Islington Avenue, #2211
Toronto, Ontario

MARIAN CROW, CKD
OAKVILLE KITCHEN CENTRE
93 Bronte Road
Oakville

JOHN HUNTER, CKD
992 Timmins Garden Road
Pickering, Ontario

DUNCAN McKERRACHER, CKD
CHATELAINE KITCHEN DESIGNS
3323B Mainway
Burlington, Ontario

GLORIA RUTHERFORD, CKD
INTERPLAN DESIGNS
203 Battle Street West
Kamloops, British Columbia

ROBERT SMYTH, CKD
LAURENTIDE KITCHENS
945 Eglinton Avenue East
Toronto, Ontario

LINDA WHALING, CKD
WHALING KITCHEN DESIGNS
518 Tenth Street
Hanover, Ontario

GORDON WILSON, CKD
DANICA CABINETS
647 Parkdale Avenue
Hamilton, Ontario

CAROLYN YOST, CKD
KITCHENS ETCETERA
275 Richmond Road
Ottawa, Ontario

General

APPRAISAL CONSTRUCTION LTD.
40 Main Street
Cornerbrook, Newfoundland

ARTISTIC KITCHENS
485 Silver Creek Parkway North
Guelph, Ontario

ARTISTIC KITCHENS
237 Tenth Street
Hanover, Ontario

BALL KITCHEN CENTRE
705 Rye Street, Unit 2
Peterborough, Ontario

BATTLERS KITCHENS
281 Braemore Avenue
Waterloo, Ontario

BECHLER KITCHENS
150 The Shoppers Square
Goderich, Ontario

BENNIE LUMBER
124 Keil Drive
Chatham, Ontario

BILT-RITE KITCHEN SHOWPLACE
818C Cynthia Street
Saskatoon, Saskatchewan

BRADFORD PLANNED KITCHENS
49 Morrow Road
Barrie, Ontario

CAMERON'S INSULATION
7 South Branch Road
Cornwall, Ontario

CARTER'S KITCHEN CENTRE
Richmond Street North
Arva (London), Ontario

CASEY'S CREATIVE KITCHENS
244 Talbot Street
St. Thomas, Ontario

CHATELAINE KITCHEN DESIGNS
3323B Mainway
Burlington, Ontario

CONTOUR KITCHEN DESIGN
5503 West Boulevard
Vancouver, British Columbia

COUNTRYWIDE KITCHENS
407 Counter Street, #110
Kingston, Ontario

COVLIN-KING INTERIORS
214 Fourth Avenue East
Regina, Saskatchewan

DREGER'S KITCHEN CORNER
10442 82nd Avenue
Edmonton, Alberta

HANOVER KITCHENS
6214 Quinpool Road
Halifax, Nova Scotia

HANOVER KITCHENS (OTTAWA)
70 Colonnade Road
Nepean, Ontario

HANOVER KITCHENS
2725 Yonge Street
Toronto, Ontario

J.F. HAZZARD & ASSOCIATES
79 Sheppard Avenue West
Toronto, Ontario

THE KITCHEN EMPORIUM
54 Kent Street
Woodstock, Ontario

THE KITCHEN PLACE
337 Kingston Road
Pickering, Ontario

KITCHENS ETCETERA
275 Richmond Road
Ottawa, Ontario

JAKE KLASSEN'S KITCHEN GALLERY
944½ Portage Avenue
Winnipeg, Manitoba

LAURENTIDE KITCHENS
945 Eglinton Avenue East
Toronto, Ontario

PAT LOW INTERIORS & CUSTOM
KITCHENS
4 Fox Street
Leamington, Ontario

McARTHUR & REILLY
1101 Second Avenue East
Owen Sound, Ontario

MERIT KITCHEN CENTRE
2401 Burrard Street
Vancouver, British Columbia

NU-WAY HOME CENTRE
226 Euston Street
Charlottetown, Prince Edward Island

OAKVILLE KITCHEN CENTRE
93 Bronte Road
Oakville, Ontario

PARKDALE KITCHENS
400 Parkdale Avenue
Hamilton, Ontario

PENISTON INDUSTRIES
301 Forest Avenue
Orillia, Ontario

W. RICKS WOODWORKING
617 Assiniboine Avenue
Brandon, Manitoba

ROMAN BATH & KITCHENS
3347 Miller Avenue
Saskatoon, Saskatchewan

SHELGAR KITCHENS
3050 Portage Avenue West
Winnipeg, Manitoba

TOWN AND COUNTRY KITCHENS
17212 107th Avenue
Edmonton, Alberta

THORNE'S KITCHEN COUNTRY
189 Lakeshore Road East
Mississauga, Ontario

PHOTOGRAPH CREDITS

Courtesy of Abbaka Trading Co., Inc.: *41 (top, center, bottom)*
Courtesy of Allmilmo: *116, 117*
Roger Bester: *89 (left, right)*
Hedrich Blessing: *17, 22, 39 (bottom), 48, 49, 65, 96*
Courtesy of Brown-Neff Ltd.: *37 (top right), 40*
Karen Bussolini: *23, 61 (right), 80, 102*
Langdon Clay: *25, 75*
Courtesy of Country Floors: *68*
Jim D'Addio: *78*
Michael Datoli: *98*
Derrick & Love: *88, 113*
Dan Eifert: *12, 15, 30, 35, 38, 56, 82, 95, 100–101, 101*
Phillip Ennis: *43, 73, 77, 92*
Courtesy of Gaggeneau Corp.: *36–37*
Joshua Greene: *44–45, 93*
Courtesy of Häfele America Co.: *46, 50*
Courtesy of House of Ceramics: *108–109*
Courtesy of Jenn-Aire: *52, 110*
Ken Kirkwood: *27, 50–51, 55, 79, 85*
Courtesy of Mannington Mills—Holophane Classics Division: *69 (left)*
Alf Martensen—Design Council: *64*

Norman McGrath: *21 (bottom), 91, 111*
Keith Scott Morton (Courtesy of Siesel Co.): *67*
Courtesy of McKone Co., Inc. for Wilsonart: *28 (right)*
Greg Moulesworth: *16 (bottom), 87 (bottom)*
Peter Paige: *14, 16, 24 (top), 59 (left), 104, 105, 115*
Robert Perron: *13, 18, 22–23, 30–31, 61 (left), 86*
Courtesy of Poggenpohl: *6, 10, 28 (left), 47 (top and bottom), 69 (left)*
Tim Street-Porter: *20, 21 (top left), 26 (left), 26–27, 29, 31, 51 (top), 58, 60, 63, 70, 97, 106, 107*
Courtesy of Quakermaid: *32*
Courtesy of Roseline Products, Inc.: *94 (left), 114*
Bill Rothschild: *11, 112*
Durston Saylor: *24 (bottom), 62, 76*
John Schwartz: *42 (top), 59 (right), 87 (top), 90, 118*
Courtesy of SieMatic: *8, 72*
Joe Standart: *83*
Courtesy of Summitville Tiles: *66, 94 (right)*
Courtesy of Thorn Emi: *37 (bottom right)*
Paul Warchol: *39 (top), 54, 62–63, 81*
Courtesy of Zanussi: *36*

DESIGN CREDITS

Stephen Ackerman—Design Collaborative: *43, 92*
Leslie Armstrong—Armstrong Cummings Architects: *11*
Andrew Batey: *29, 97*
Eric Bernard Designs: *16 (bottom), 87 (bottom)*
Ryall Bishop, architect: *25*
Susan Bishop: *93*
Pierre Botschi: *79*
John Canning, artist: *61 (right)*
Eric Chase, architect: *80*
George Constant: *113 (right)*
James Cornish, architect: *27 (right)*
Charles Damga: *82–83*
Rubin DeSaavedra: *15*
Dail Dixon: *22–23 (center)*
William Norton—18th Century Co.: *102–103*
Rita Falkner: *35, 38*
Peg Gorson: *105*
Frank Gehry, architect: *26–27 (center)*
Gilvarg/Epstien: *23 (right)*
Goshow Associates: *88*
Piers Gough, architect: *63 (right)*
Glenn Gregg: *30–31 (center)*
Michael Hopkins: *85*
HQ2 Enterprises: *24 (top)*
Steven Hubberman: *112–113*
Norman Jaffe: *21 (bottom)*
David James, architect: *70–71*
Jan Kaplicky: *55*
Kips Bay: *16 (top)*

Doris Laporte: *81*
Paul Leonard: *67*
Jack Lowery: *89 (left and right)*
Louis MacKall: *18–19*
Sandy Moore, artist: *61 (left)*
Richard Neas: *100–101, 101*
Lyn Peterson—Motif Designs: *73 (right)*
Andrew Pettit: *78*
Antoine Prudock: *51 (top)*
Pat Radlauer, A.S.I.D.: *11*
Joseph Roman: *95*
Shelly and Janet Rosenberg: *62 (left), 76*
Michael Rubin and Henry Smith-Miller: *91*
David Rubino: *50–51 (center)*
St. Charles Kitchens: *42 (top), 59 (right), 87 (top), 90, 118*
Peter Shire, table designer: *60*
Shope, Reno, Wharton: *24 (bottom)*
Charles Sieger: *86*
Barry Sloane: *58*
Jay Spectre: *75*
Katherine Stephens for Kips Bay: *12*
Studio 55: *114–115*
Mojo Stumer, architects: *77*
Calvin Tsao: *54*
David Webster: *98–99*
Allee Willis: *106*
David Witcomb: *56–57, 82–83*
Stuart Wrede: *61 (left)*
Buzz Yudell, architect: *107*